George Evans

An Essay on Assyriology

George Evans

An Essay on Assyriology

ISBN/EAN: 9783337235840

Printed in Europe, USA, Canada, Australia, Japan

Cover: Foto ©Thomas Meinert / pixelio.de

More available books at **www.hansebooks.com**

AN ESSAY

ON

ASSYRIOLOGY.

BY

GEORGE EVANS, M.A.

HIBBERT FELLOW.

Published by the Hibbert Trustees.

WILLIAMS AND NORGATE,

14, HENRIETTA STREET, COVENT GARDEN, LONDON;

AND 20, SOUTH FREDERICK STREET, EDINBURGH.

1883.

CONTENTS.

	PAGE
The Character of the Assyrian Language	1
The Place of Assyrian among the Semitic Languages	21
Influence of Assyrian on Hebrew Grammar	23
Influence of Assyrian on Hebrew Lexicography	27
Biblical Geography	37
Biblical History	52
Appendix	60
An Assyrian Tablet *to face page*	60
Notes	61

AN ESSAY ON ASSYRIOLOGY.

THE CHARACTER OF THE ASSYRIAN LANGUAGE.

THE Assyrian language is that which was spoken in Mesopotamia, on the banks of the Euphrates and Tigris, more than 2,000 years before Christ, by a Semitic people whom we call Assyrians, both on the authority of the Old Testament and of the Inscriptions. It continued to be a living language in this district till after the fall of Babylon (506 B.C.), and even down to the time of the Achæmenian kings in the second century B.C. The Semitic character of this language has been disputed by Renan in his "Les Langues Semitiques," and also by Hitzig and others. Hitzig derives the name Sennacherib not from any Semitic language, but from the Sanskrit, thus:—Sennacherib = συν, 'with' + *hari* (Sanskrit), 'lion' + *baha* (Sanskrit), 'daring,' 'shining' But why go to Sanskrit and Greek to explain the name of an Assyrian king? My readers, I doubt not, will agree with me that it is far more probable that the name is to be explained by the language of that people over whom he reigned. It is true that scholars in Assyrian do not thoroughly agree as to the proper explanation of the name: they are all at one as to the explanation of the first two parts of the name, but the difficulty lies with the third part. In the extract at the end of this essay you will find the word Sennacherib written ideographically, and represented by three characters. The first is the name of the moon-god *Sin;* the second is the ideograph for 'brother,' with the sign of the plural number, and is to be read *aḫê;* and the third is the ideograph 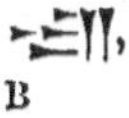, in regard to the reading of which the difficulty is. Schrader, in his "Keilinschriften und das Alte Testament," reads *irib*, from the verb 'rabû,' *to be great*, or 'to increase;' so that, according to him, the name means, "Sin has increased the brothers." Others think of the word *êribu*, or some such word, and explain it: "Sin, my brothers are come down, *i.e.*, from above." At any rate, this much is clear, that the key for explaining the name is to be got from the Assyrian. Again, Hitzig compares the well-known name שִׁנְעָר, the *Sumêr* of the Inscriptions, with the Sanskrit *Sinhaladvîpa;* and according to the same commentator, Sardanapalus, whose Assyrian name is Assurbanipal = *Sardana*, 'the heart' + *pala*, 'the protector.' Assurbanipal means "the god Assur has begotten a son." And the Assyrian language, from which these proper names are taken, is a Semitic language, and not an Indian language, as would be supposed from the explanation of Assyrian names as given by Hitzig.

Gesenius in his Grammar (*see* second English edition, pp. 3, *sqq.*) sums up the characteristics of the Semitic languages under two heads, dealing (1) with the grammatical structure, and (2) with the lexicography. We shall proceed to apply his canons to our language, and we shall thus find out how far we are justified in calling Assyrian a Semitic language.

A.—Grammatical Structure.

1. "Among the consonants which in general form the pith and substance of these languages, we find many gutturals of different gradations." In Assyrian the letter Elif ἰ (*cf.* Haupt, "Sumerische Familiengesetze," p. 20) is of five kinds. Dr. Haupt gives the following examples in proof of his statement:—ἰ$_1$ is the *a* we find in *'abu*, 'father' (אָב); ἰ$_2$ the *a* in *alâku*, 'to go' (הָלַךְ); ἰ$_3$ the *a* in *alibu*, 'sweet milk' (חָלָב); ἰ$_4$ the *a* in *aḳrâbu*, 'scorpion' (עַקְרָב); ἰ$_5$ in *uzalu*, 'gazelle' (غَزَالٌ). The student will observe that the initial *a* in the Assyrian words is represented by five different gutturals in the two other Semitic languages I have quoted. ἰ$_1$ or a_1 is

represented by א; a_2 by ה; a_3 by ח; a_4 by ע; a_5 by غ, *i.e.*, $ע_2$, the Ayin which we find in the Hebrew name of the town Gaza. Gesenius goes on to say that "the vowels proceed all from the three primary sounds (*a*, *i*, *u*), and serve to mark more subordinate distinctions." The three vowel sounds are preserved in their original purity in Assyrian: *cf.* מְאֹד with *ma'du*, 'much, many;' *ki* with כִּי, 'when.'

2. "Word-stems generally consisting of three consonants." I need hardly prove that this holds true in Assyrian, because the student can find this to be the case by simply glancing through any table of Assyrian words that has as yet been drawn up. (See, *e.g.*, the Syllabary in Sayce's Grammar.) Of course there are in it quadriliterals, as in the other Semitic languages: *cf.* a verb whose consonants are *p.r.š.d.*, and which means 'to escape.'

3. "In the Verb only two tense forms, each having a peculiarly marked-out usage, and a pervading regularity in the formation of verbals." In Assyrian there are only two tenses, viz., the Imperfect and the Present. The Imperfect has an aorist signification, and the Present an imperfect, thus: *ikšud*, 'he conquered;' *ikašud*, 'he conquers.' The pervading characteristic of the Present is an accented *a* after the first radical; in *ikašud* or *ikaššud* the radicals are *k š d*, *i.e.*, כשׁד, and after the first radical we have the vowel *a*. In *išaḳal* (שׁקל), 'he weighs,' *a* follows שׁ; so in *imádad* or *imaddad*, 'he measures.' In the Imperfect the vowel is generally *u*, thus: *imdud*, 'he measured;' *išḳul*, 'he weighed;' *ikšud*, 'he conquered;' but *a* in *ilmad*, 'he learned.'

4. "In the Noun only two genders, Masculine and Feminine." The Assyrian also only knows two genders. Its feminine in Nouns is generally formed by the addition of the syllable *tu*, thus: *kalbu*, 'a dog;' *kalbatu*, 'a bitch;' *maliku*, 'a prince;' *malkatu*, 'a princess;' *bêlu*, 'a lord;' *bêl(i)tu*, 'a lady,' &c. In Assyrian the neuter gender is impossible, and is not to be found. The Assyrian Noun has three vowel endings corresponding to the three primary vowels, viz., *u* or *um*, *i* or *im*, *a* or *am*. As in Arabic we

have the nunation, so in Assyrian we have mimation. I speak only of the *vowel-endings* of the Nouns, and not of their *cases*, because in Assyrian no fixed rule can be given in regard to the vowel-endings of the cases: *e.g.*, 'the house of the father' may be written either *bît âbi*, or *bîtu ša âbi* (not *bîti âbi*, because *bîti* s estr. state): rarely *bît ša âbi*. The use of the particle *ša* in these examples to express a genitival relationship corresponds to the use of the ܕ in Syriac, דְ in Aramaic, and ዘ in Æthiopic.

5. "In the Pronoun the oblique cases indicated by appended forms (*suffixa*)." The Assyrian has both *nominal* and *verbal* suffixes. (*a*) Nominal suffixes, *e.g.*, *âbî* or *âbi-ia*, *i.e.*, *âbîa*, 'my father;' *âbī-ka*, 'thy father;' *âbī-šu*, 'his father;' *ziru-ni*, 'our race;' *libbi-kun* (pl.), 'your heart;' *šarri-šunu*, 'their king.' (*b*) The verbal suffixes are—

Singular	1st Person			= *-anni* or *-inni*.
	2nd	,,		= *-ka*, *-akka*, or *-ikka*.
	3rd	,,	(masc.)	= *-šu*.
	3rd	,,	(fem.)	= *-ši*.
Plural	1st Person			= *-annâši*.
	2nd	,,		= *kunu*, *-kunuši*.
	3rd	,,	(masc.)	= *-šun*, *šunûtu*, *šunûti*, or *šunûši*.
	3rd	,,	(fem.)	= *šin*, *šinâ*, &c.

6. "Scarcely any compounds, either in the Noun (except many proper names) or in the Verb." This canon holds especially true of Assyrian, compounds being largely limited to the proper names, *e.g.*, *Tiglathpileser* = *Tugulti-apil-ešarra*; *Esarhaddon* = *Aššur-aḫu-iddina*; *Nebuchadnezzar* = *Nabû-kudurri-uṣur*. There are cases, undoubtedly, of compound words other than proper names, *e.g.*, *ašarîdu*, 'the chief' = *ašar* (construct state of *ašru*, 'a place') + *idu*, 'the first,' so that *ašarîdu* means 'the first in place or rank.'

7. In proof that Gesenius's 7th canon, "in the syntax a simple succession of clauses without much periodic structure in the sentences," holds in Assyrian, I need only refer the student to any of the historical translations in the Assyrian volumes of the "Records of the Past."

B.—The Lexicography.

In Assyrian, as in other Semitic languages, there is a large foreign element, larger perhaps than in the others, chiefly on account of the character of the Assyrian people. In Syriac there are a large number of words borrowed from the Greek and Latin; and in Æthiopic, of words borrowed from the Greek.

1. So in Assyrian we have words borrowed from the non-Semitic Akkadian language, besides other ancient languages, the existence of which admits no longer of any doubt. We are now fully convinced that in the Cuneiform inscriptions of Western Asia we have not only the Assyrian, Akkadian, and Sumerian languages, but also some others, about which we can say little at present. Words borrowed from the Akkadian are the following: *êkallu* (הֵיכָל), 'a palace,' from the Akkadian *ê*, 'a house' + *gal*, 'great,' *i.e.*, from *êgal; ḳanu*, 'a reed,' from *gên; agarinnu*, 'the mother;' *agû*, 'crown,' from *agá*, and many others.

2. There also exist in Assyrian a number of words which are either entirely wanting in the other Semitic languages, or only traces of which can be discovered in them. Examples of these are the prepositions *ana* and *ina*, and the verb *êpîšu*, 'to make.' A large number of words can have their meanings fixed only from the syllabaries, as being synonyms of words whose meaning is already known. A most interesting confirmation of this statement can be found in the Rassam Fragment, quoted by Delitzsch in Lotz's "Tiglathpileser," pp. 88 and 89. There, as synonyms of *šarru*, 'a king,' are given: *ma-al-ku, ma-li-ku, lu-li-mu, pa-rak-ku, ê-til-lu;* as synonyms of *bêlu*, 'a lord,' we have *ri'u* and *ê-nu*. In line 11, as synonym of *šarratu*, 'a queen,' we have *ma-al-ka-tu*. *Cf.* further II R, plate 31, No. 3, first five words.

3. The greater number of Assyrian words have a close relationship with the words in Hebrew and Aramaic, Æthiopic and Arabic. For words to be compared with the Hebrew,

see the part of this Essay which treats of the influence of Assyrian on Hebrew Lexicography.

ARAMAIC.	*mâtu*,	'land'	= מָתָא
	šinuntu,	'the swallow'	= סְנוּנִיתָא [ܣܢܘܢܝܬܐ]
	mûtânu,	'plague'	= מוֹתָנָא
	titurru,	'the bridge'	= תִּיתּוּרָא
	abullu,	'the city-gate'	= אַבּוּלָא
SYRIAC.	*elippu*,	'the ship'	= ܐܠܦܐ
	imêru,	'the ass'	= ܚܡܪܐ
	aḳrabu,	'the scorpion'	= ܥܩܪܒܐ
	šêdu,	'the demon'	= ܫܐܕܐ
ÆTHIOPIC.	*kišâdu*,	'the neck'	= ክሳድ፡
	mutu,	'the man'	= ምት፡
	ṣâbu,	'the warrior'	= ጸበኢ፡
ARABIC.	*ruḳḳu*,	'firmament'	= رقع (*cf.* רקיע)
	ṣirtu,	'the female breast'	= صرع
	šimtum,	'fate'	= شيمة
	nubtum,	'bee'	= نوبة

These proofs seem to me sufficient to establish my assertion, that the Assyrian is to be classed among the Semitic languages, as first asserted by the Swede Löwenstern in 1845.

Already in the beginning of the seventeenth century travellers informed us of the existence of rare inscriptions which they had seen in the ruins of Persepolis and in other places. As drawings of them were brought to Europe, people at once endeavoured to decipher them. But the kind of writing in the copies, with the wedge as its fundamental element, was to them perfectly new; and so it happened that in spite of frequent attempts at decipherment they remained for two hundred years a dead letter, and it appeared as if they must always remain so. However, towards the end of the eighteenth century new copies, easier of access, came to Europe, and happily the attempt at decipherment was soon crowned with success. The elder Niebuhr was the first who published exact copies of the Persian Cuneiform inscriptions, and Tychsen, of Rostock, in 1798, rightly conjectured that the characters were alphabetical, and were to be read from left to right. In September, 1802, Georg Friedrich Grotefend, from the Gymnasium at Hanover, published a translation of an old Persian Cuneiform text. He first of all showed that the Cuneiform writing was a writing and not an ornament, as might have been supposed. What distinguished it from all other sorts of writing was the utter absence of roundness in the characters, which made it excellently adapted for cutting upon stone. This writing Grotefend set about deciphering. He took in hand two small inscriptions in the Persian Cuneiform character. He had learnt from old authors that the palaces at Persepolis, on whose ruins these two inscriptions were found, had been built by Achæmenian kings. Münter had already happily guessed that one word which occurred often in the inscriptions was the word for *king*, and he was right. This same word happened to occur also in the two inscriptions upon which Grotefend was engaged. These two were almost exactly like one another, the difference consisting only in this, that in the first inscription a group of signs A preceded the word for *king*, in the second inscription a group of signs B preceded; and that, further, at the end of the second inscription, the group of signs A and the word for *king* occurred, while in the first inscription a group of signs C, without the word for *king*, was at the end. The inscriptions had therefore these forms:—

	Group of signs.		Group of signs.	
First inscription ..	A	king	C	—
Second inscription ..	B	king	A	king

Grotefend concluded that these groups of signs must be proper names which stood in genealogical relationship to one another. A must be the father of B, C the father of A. He saw that A and B were kings, but that C was not, because the title was wanting after his name. He then inferred that A was the founder of a dynasty. He knew the names of the Achæmenian kings, and his task now was to find out the names of the kings corresponding to A, B, C. "Fully convinced," says Grotefend, "that here two kings of the Achæmenian dynasty must be sought for, and finding the history of the Greeks as their contemporaries and narrators of contemporary events the most reliable, I began at once to go through the list of kings, and to examine which names allied themselves most easily to the characters in the inscriptions. They could not be Cyrus and Cambyses, because the two names on the inscriptions did not begin with the same letter; nor could they be Cyrus and Artaxerxes, because the first name, Cyrus, was too short in proportion to the characters on the inscription, and the name Artaxerxes was too long. There remained then only the names Darius and Xerxes, which suited the characters well." And besides, it is to be noticed that there was another reason for saying it could not be Cyrus, viz., the father and son of Cyrus had the same name, viz., Cambyses, while on the inscriptions B and C were different. Grotefend thus inferred that A was Darius. Beginning with the well-known Greek, Hebrew, and Persian forms of the name, he read:—

A. D-a-r-h-w-u-sch.
B. Kh-sch-h-a-r-sch-a.
C. V-i-sch-t-a-s-p.

Subsequent investigations have shown that he had read correctly, except that for *h* he ought to have read *j*. In this way a certain number of letters was ascertained, and the word for king could now be read. Grotefend thus laid down the foundation of the decipherment of the Persian Cuneiform inscriptions. There now came a period of about thirty years during which no progress was made in the work which

Grotefend had begun. In 1836 appeared two works from the pens of the French scholar, Eugene Burnouf, and the Bonn Professor, Christian Lassen, which showed a marked advance on the work of Grotefend. Lassen corrected the results of his predecessors, and made an alphabetical list of some thirty-nine characters. Lassen's work began by acknowledging that Grotefend had given us an alphabet by means of which we had been able to recognize the names Darius, Xerxes, and Hystaspes, and he further acknowledged that by means of it the word which meant 'king,' as well as another meaning 'lands,' had been read. This was, however, all that had been done. He then showed that Grotefend's alphabet was only partly correct. Distinguishing between what was undoubtedly correct and what admitted of doubt, he proceeds to say: "As there was no longer any doubt that the names of the kings had been correctly read, so it was clear that the value of the letters in the names had been correctly fixed." Grotefend failed, however, to advance, in that he assumed that the old Persian and the Awesta dialects were perfectly identical, while, in fact, both were distinct from one another. Lassen saw this mistake, and thus he was able to go further on in the work than Grotefend. With the help of his more perfect alphabet he ventured to read and to explain the old Persian Cuneiform texts.

Just at this time a young English officer, now Sir Henry Rawlinson, was engaged on the same work. He brought new materials to light by the discovery of the sculptured tablets of Hamadan (which he copied), and of the long Behistun Inscription. Not far from the town of Kermanschah was a steep mountain called Behistun, about 1,700 feet high, into the rock of which was cut an inscription of Darius Hystaspes, consisting of about 400 lines, and which was about 300 feet from the ground. The inscription was a little damaged by the water of a small stream which trickled down the rocky side of the mountain and over the inscription. To get at this was no easy task. The indomitable pluck of the English officer surmounted all difficulties: he not only copied it for the first time, between the years 1835 and 1837, but to the learned officer belongs the honour of having first given a translation of the same in 1846.

On the Achæmenian inscriptions, side by side with the Persian Cuneiform inscriptions, were two others, also in the Cuneiform characters. Grotefend had expressed the opinion that these two were translations of the first (the Persian) into two languages, which at some time had been spoken in Persia. This proved to be a correct conjecture. It is clear that the Persian princes would wish their inscriptions to be read by all their subjects, and hence it was that they appeared in these three languages. The proper names which occurred so frequently in the Persian texts enabled the decipherer to read the inscriptions that stood at their side; it was found that the large number of wedges which these two new languages contained was due to the fact that here were languages which were not written alphabetically, but syllabically. Each of the characters denoted a syllable, and not a letter. It was conjectured that the third language in the group of Achæmenian inscriptions was that of Babylonia and Assyria, and this conjecture was right. For just at this time excavations had been begun in Assyria, and inscriptions were brought to light, whose writing corresponded exactly with that which was on the old Achæmenian inscriptions as the third. The site of Ninivch was first excavated by Botta, and then by Layard (Sir Henry Austin Layard). Here were now brought forth into the light of day inscriptions which had been hidden for centuries—tablets, cylinders, foundations of temples and palaces, obelisks, &c. It was now evident that the deciphering of these would only be a work of time. The Greek translation upon the Rosetta Stone was to the decipherer of the Egyptian text, what the old Persian inscriptions were to be to the decipherer of the Babylonian-Assyrian inscriptions. Fortunately there were preserved on the old Persian monuments ninety proper names phonetically written in the Persian character of the trilingual Achæmenian inscriptions, and it was clear that with this help success must soon crown the efforts of scholars to read the third language.

It was observed that the names of persons, gods, lands, trees, &c., on these newly discovered inscriptions, had a determining sign always prefixed to them. There was a certain sign prefixed to all names of gods (viz., 𒀭), and another sign to all names of lands (viz., 𒆳), and so on. Having gained this much, Dr. Hincks saw that this new language was not alphabetic in its character. He was the first to discover that it was written syllabically and ideographically. He soon found himself able to read the name of Nebuchadnezzar, and the record of his buildings. The untiring labours of Hincks, Oppert, Menant, and others, were successful in overcoming most of the difficulties which the polyphonic nature of the single characters had caused to be in the way of the decipherer. Since the labours of the first decipherers, the path of the Assyrian scholar has been smoother, and now we may say that the foundation of the work of deciphering Assyrian inscriptions has been firmly laid. (*See* Appendix, Note 1.)

The Assyrian is originally a language in picture-writing, like the Egyptian. This is easily seen by glancing over the first few pages of the 1st volume of the "Cuneiform Inscriptions of Western Asia" (to which volumes I shall henceforth refer thus: I R for the 1st volume; II R for the 2nd; III R, &c.; *i.e.*, 1st Rawlinson, &c.). In the late Assyrian writing it is often possible to trace the relationship between certain groups of signs and their original representatives in the picture-writing, *e.g.*, hieratic 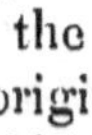, old Babylonian 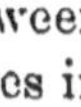, later Assyrian 𒀭, an ideograph for 'a star;' again, hieratic 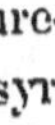, old Babylonian 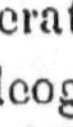, later Assyrian 𒋗, ideograph for 'hand;' hieratic 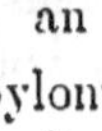, old Babylonian , later Assyrian 𒌓, ideograph for 'sun.' Sometimes two of these are joined together in order to form a new sign, *e.g.*,  'sun, day,' is joined to 𒌍, the sign for the numeral 30, to form the new sign , which means 'a month,' *i.e.*, day + 30 = 30 days, 'a month.' From the Assyrian 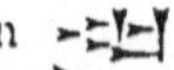 'the mouth' +  'water,' we have the ideograph 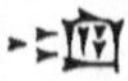 'to drink.'  'the mouth' +  'the sun' = 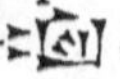 *ṣûmu*, 'thirst.' This system of writing the Babylonians and Assyrians received from the older inhabitants, the Sumerians and Akkadians. Not only were the old signs retained by the former, but also the meanings attached to these. These meanings were afterwards used either as borrowed words or as syllabic values: thus:  in Akkadian = *ana*, 'the heaven,' which appears in Assyrian as *an*, the syllabic value of this sign. Again, has the value *bat* in Assyrian, from the Akkadian word *bat*, 'to open;' also the value *til*, from the Akkadian *til*, 'to be ready, completed;'  *maš*, from the Akkadian word *maš*, 'the wilderness.' The Assyrians also gave to their signs values which were not borrowed from these older non-Semitic languages, but values which were taken from the Semitic languages. Thus  means 'a house;' so they gave this character the value *bit*, corresponding to the Hebrew בַּיִת; and to  the value *rêš*, corresponding to the Hebrew ראשׁ 'head.'

The Assyrian writing is in the Cuneiform character, and consists of combinations of wedges and corner-wedges (<). These wedges are either horizontal, perpendicular, or oblique. Like the other Cuneiform writings, such as the Persian, Median, Armenian and Elamitic, the Assyrian writing reads from left to right. A syllable may consist of a combination of wedges varying from the single wedge up to a compound of even twenty. Thus we have the single wedges 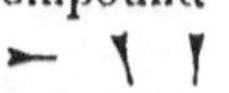 and the corner-wedge <, and from these are formed combinations varying in complexity. This will be clear to the student if he will only examine any volume in the Assyrian writing.

In regard to the nature of the Assyrian characters, it is to be remarked that they are syllabic and ideographic, in contradistinction to the old Persian, which are alphabetic (the other Semitic languages, such as Hebrew, Arabic, Syriac, Æthopic, having consonantal characters). That is to say, the single Cuneiform characters in Assyrian may be read either as syllables, thus: 𒈾 = *na*, and 𒅗 = *ka*; or as representing an idea, and therefore to be treated as being equal to a word in value: thus, 𒅗, whose syllabic value is *ka*, has the ideographic value *pû*, which means 'mouth,' the Hebrew פֶּה.

There are also in Assyrian both *open* syllables, such as *ka*, *ki*, *ku*, and closed syllables, which are really compound syllables, as *kar*, *kir*, *kur*, i.e., *ka*+*ar*, *ki*+*ir*, *ku-ur*. I call them compound, because in writing the closed syllable *kar*, the Assyrians might use two characters representing two syllables, viz., the characters whose values are respectively *ka* and *ar*. A character may also have many phonetic or syllabic values as well as many ideographic values. Thus 𒁁 has the syllabic values *bê*, *bat*, *mit*, *til*, *ziz*; and the ideographic values *pitû*, 'to open;' *ḳatû*, 'to be completed;' *gamru*, 'complete;' *bêlu*, 'lord;' *kabtu*, 'heavy;' *labiru*, 'old;' *dâmu*, 'blood,' and some others; 𒅗, whose only syllabic value is *ka*, has the ideographic values *pû*, 'the mouth;' *appu*, 'the face;' *šinnu*, 'a tooth;' *kibitu*, 'a command;' *amâtu*, 'a word;' *rigmu*, 'a cry;' *ragâmu*, 'to speak,' &c., &c.

In the various tables of signs which we find in the works of modern scholars who write on Assyrian, a clear method of arrangement is observed. It is clear that the various combinations of characters fall naturally into certain groups, according to the kind of wedge which stands first on the left side of the character. Thus 𒀭 must be placed under the 𒀸 group; 𒀹, under the 𒀹 group; 𒌋, under the 𒌋 group; and 𒁹, under the 𒁹 group. Of course there is an obvious advantage to the beginner in such an arrangement. The order in which these four groups stand in the various tables of signs drawn up by grammarians varies according to the will of the author. The order in Sayce's Grammar is very much the same as that adopted by Delitzsch and Haupt; in some of the French works the student will find other arrangements adopted.

In looking over the table, the student observes that a character may have several values, *e.g.*, 𒉌 has the values of *ni, zal, ṣal, ili.* How do we know which of these to take when we are transcribing a passage? As stated above, a word may be written syllabically, thus *na-da-nu*, or the word *nadanu* may be represented by its ideograph 𒋧. In a syllabically-written work, our choice of a value may be made with tolerable certainty if we attend to the following rule:—"*The one syllable must end with the same letter with which the other begins.*" Of course this does not always lead us to a correct result. To the word *na-da-nu* we see this rule does not apply at all: the characters for *na* and *nu* have only these values, so that no doubt can arise here about the values; and the character for *da*, viz., 𒁕, has only the values *da* and *ṭa* (viz., ט). The student will find that the above rule is a good one to use whenever he is in difficulty. But a constant study of the inscriptions alone, I am convinced, can give one ease in transcribing correctly, *i.e.*, in choosing values correctly. In many cases it is not so easy to select the values, as in *nadanu*, and the best help which the student can have in selecting will be to have as good an acquaintance as possible with the other Semitic languages. A fair acquaintance with these is absolutely necessary to the Assyrian scholar, because words in them will often suggest a correct reading of a sign, and also give a clue to the meaning of the Assyrian word.

Having learnt to transcribe well, the student must learn to translate. Transcribing well must first be thoroughly learnt, and to do the work of translating well the student will have to work at the other Semitic languages, and at the numerous syllabaries given in the "Cuneiform Inscriptions of Western Asia." It will be found that these syllabaries are very much broken. An examination of the original tablets in the British Museum will show to the reader in what a mutilated condition many of these are. Still, many of them are well preserved, and these have been copied with moderate accuracy into the volumes I have recommended to the student for reading. A syllabary may be defined as *a cata-*

logue of words syllabically written, containing on one side of the character whose values these words represent, the Assyrian equivalents, and on the other side, the Akkadian and Sumerian equivalents corresponding to them. For an advanced student of Assyrian, a careful study of these syllabaries is necessary, but for a beginner I would suggest that the syllabaries in Professor Delitzsch's "Lesestücke," and designated by him S^a, S^b, S^c, which are, in fact, collections from the "Cuneiform Inscriptions of Western Asia," would be an invaluable study. The student really has no complete Assyrian dictionary before him (for Mr. Norris's, which was prepared at a time when the study of Assyrian had not made so much progress as at the present day, can hardly be regarded as altogether reliable) such as the student of the other Semitic languages has, and the only dictionary he may be said to have are these syllabaries: an excellent dictionary indeed to the careful student.

These syllabaries are of various kinds. For example, II R, plate 3, lines 537–566 (which we also have in Delitzsch's "Lesestücke," under S^a, column iii, 1–30, with many gaps filled up by the Professor from comparison with other parts of the Cuneiform Inscriptions of Western Asia), contains three columns. In the middle column is the character whose conventional name is given in the right-hand column, and whose various syllabic values are given in the left-hand one. Thus , lines 551–554, has in the right-hand column the name *Gu-ru-šú*; in the left-hand column it is seen to have the syllabic values *dan, kal, lib* or *lip* and *guruš*. Further on, in lines 560–564,  has the name *gêltanû*, and the values *pi, mé, tal, gêltan*. To one already acquainted with Assyrian, it will occur that, *e.g.*,  has oftenest the values *dan* and *kal*: *guruš* is in reality its Akkadian value. Again, , in II R 3, 518–523, has the name *kuru*, and the values *kur, šad* or *šat, lad* or *lat, mad* or *mat*, values well known to belong to this character.

There is another kind of syllabary, in the middle column of which is the character; in the right-hand column are the Assyrian words which represent the values of the thoughts contained in it; in the left-hand column are the corresponding Akkadian or Sumerian equivalents. Thus, in II R 1, 172, 173, we have in the middle column the character 𒆗, its Assyrian rendering is *aḳru*, 'precious' (*cf.* יָקָר); and *êtlu*, which means 'high, a hero;' in the left-hand column are the Akkadian words corresponding to these: *kala* is Akkadian for *aḳru*, and *guruš* for *êtlu*. In Delitzsch's "Lesestücke" the syllabary S[b] is of this kind.

We have yet one other kind of syllabary exemplified in S[c] of Delitzsch's "Lesestücke." This is a combination of the other two kinds of syllabaries. It has four columns:—

In the 2nd column is the character to be explained.
In the 3rd column is its conventional name.
In the 4th column is its Assyrian value.
In the 1st column is its Akkadian or Sumerian value.

Cf. IV R, plates 69 and 70. We shall again take the sign, 𒆗 (IV R 70, 26). The character stands in the 2nd column. In the 3rd column is its name, viz., *gu*-[*ru-šú*]. [The student observes that we have in this plate only the beginning of the name preserved, viz., *gu*. In II R 3, 551–554, it has the name *gu-ru-šú*. We know, therefore, from this how to fill up the gap in IV R 70, 26, viz., by adding *ru-šú*, *i.e.*, 𒊒𒋙.] In the 4th column we have the Assyrian renderings of this character, viz., *aḳ-su*, 'mighty;' *aštu*, 'mighty;' *dannu*, 'mighty;' *aḳru*, 'precious,' &c. The student will remember that the value *aḳru* was also given to it in II R 1, 172. In the 1st column is given the Akkadian rendering, viz., *kala*, a value it also had in II R 1, 172.

Suppose we now take up an inscription to read it. We find that it consists of several detached groups of signs. These may be read either syllabically or ideographically. We learn from the first kind of syllabary what syllabic value to give to each group of signs, and from the other two kinds of syllabaries the ideographic values. In order to make my meaning plain, I shall take up the inscription of Assurnazirpal. I R, plates 17, *sq.*, and read line 54, where we shall find that, in order to get the true sense of the line, some of the characters must be read ideographically, but most of them syllabically, thus :—

Ab-bul a-ḳur ina išâti àšr-up ištu mât Num-mê. The first character I read *ab:* it has also the value *ap;* the next character is *bul,* which also has the value *pul.* I accept the values in *b,* because I know of a verb *nabâlu,* 'to destroy,' which gives the sense I require in this passage. Next comes a character which has the value *a;* the next the value *ḳur,* and thus we have the word *aḳur = aḳḳur,* from *naḳâru,* 'to lay waste.' Then comes a character having the values *aš* and *rum,* but also having the ideographic value *ina,* the preposition 'in.' This suits the passage, and so we read *ina.* The next character has the values *nê, tê,* &c.; but shall we have good sense if we take the syllabic value? We find that we shall not. And so, as with the former character, we must here also take the ideographic value of the character. It is known to have the value *išâti* (*cf.* אֵשׁ, Syriac ܐܫܬܐ, and the Æthiopic *ĕsât*), 'fire.' This value we accept. Then comes a character which is the sign for the plural number. This shows us that the character which preceded this sign of the plural was to be read ideographically, and also that the value given to it must be a noun. We see then that our reading *išâti* must be correct. The next character, , has no syllabic value. We know, however, from the syllabaries that it has the ideographic value *šarâpu* (שָׂרַף), 'to burn.' This suits the context. The character that follows has the values *ub, up, ar.* We take this to be a *Phonetic Complement,* *i.e.,* we accept that value of it which suits as the final syllable of the word *šarâpu,* and we read the two characters thus: *àšr-up,* i.e., *ašrup,* the Imperfect 1st Person Singular of the verb, and meaning 'I burnt.' The next character has the value *ta;* but the student observes that beneath it is given a *Variant, i.e., the exact equivalent either syllabically or ideographically of the character given in the text.* This may serve as a definition of variant which holds generally good. Sometimes a variant only tells the reader how the final vowel of a syllable is to be read, thus, to read *tê* and not *ti.* The character in the text we are told by the variant to read by its ideographic value, *iš-tu.* We know from the context that the syllabic value would not suit, and the variant decides for us what we shall read. *Ištu* is a preposition, and means *ex,* 'out of.' The next character has many syllabic values, but we also know that it has many ideographic values, such as *mâtu,* 'land,' *šadû,* 'mountain,' &c. Here our character is a *Determinative Prefix,* determining for us the character of the two signs which follow. We read the value *mât,* 'land.' The next two characters we read syllabically, thus, *Num-mê,* the name of the land. The whole line reads as follows:—

ab-bul	a-ḳur	ina išâti	âšr-up	ištu mat Num-mê, &c.
I destroyed,	*I wasted,*	*in fire*	*I burnt:*	*out of the land Nummê, &c.*

The student will have observed in the above line the occurrence of what is called a variant, and we cannot, I think, too highly estimate the value of variants. These often prove the correctness of the values which have been given to the various characters. I think we may with advantage take the above-mentioned Inscription of Assurnazirpal, and examine the nature of the variants given on the first page:—

Line 1. 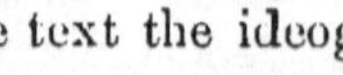. Here we have the Determinative Prefix *ilu,* 'god,' showing that the two characters which follow form the name of a god, viz., Nin-ip. The variant 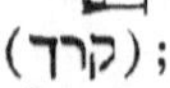 is equivalent to this. In it we have the Determinative and the character , which, according to IV R, plate 69, is the god Ninip. Compare line 10 of this plate, where we have in the text the ideographic writing, and in the variant the syllabic.

. Here the variant reads syllabically *ḳar-du* (קרד); and *ḳardu* is the ideographic value of the two characters in the text. In Dr. Haupt's "Akkadische and Sumerische Keilschrifttexte," Part 1, page 35, and No. 852, the Assyrian value of this ideograph is given *ḳar-(ra)-du.*

Let the reader look at line 32 of our plate (1 R 17); we read for the same two characters which are in this line the variant *ḳar-ra-da*. This *ḳarradu* + the following *ku* = *ḳarradaku* = *karradu anaku*, i.e., 'I (am) strong.'

Line 2. The text reads *tu-ḳu*, and the variant is *tuḳ*. This shows that the variant character has not only the value it generally has, viz., *tuk*, but also *tuḳ* (i.e., ק). In line 3 the text has *tim*, and the variant is *ti*. In line 4 text has *u*, and the variant is *ú*.

Line 5. As a variant for 𒂊 *é*, is given the plural sign 𒈨𒌍. The character which precedes *é* means *bêlu*, 'lord.' The variant shows that we have to read the plural of this word in the text, and the syllable *é* shows that the plural ending is *é:* plural = *bêlê*. In the text the repetition of the character shows that the ideograph is to be in the plural. *Cf.* with this the usage in Syriac, where repetition denotes diversity or multitude (*cf.* Nöldeke's "Syrische Grammatik," p. 137, or Phillips' "Syriac Grammar," p. 140). The advanced student in Assyrian will have remarked that the plural of a large class of nouns ends in *é*. Further on in line 5, as a variant of 𒀭 ($^{pad}_{pat}$), is given $pa + ^{ad}_{at}$, i.e., *pad* or *pat*.

Line 10. The text reads *arba'-i;* the variant shows that we may read *irbit-ta*. The former is feminine, the latter masculine. (*Cf.* Sayce's "Grammar," p. 55.) Both *i* and *ta* are Phonetic Complements.

Line 18. Text reads *a-na* (preposition = *to*). We know that 𒁹 is a common ideograph for *ana*. *Cf.* the first character in this inscription.

Line 19. 𒈗, the usual ideograph for *šarru*, 'a king.' As its variant is given 𒌋𒌋. In line 14 this variant has the value *niš*, its syllabic value, and in line 19 we see that *šarru* is its ideographic value. In line 32, 𒌋𒌋 = *šar-ra* in the text, viz., the accusative case of *šarru*. Again, in this line 19, text reads *pi-ir*, i.e., *pir*, showing that the variant 𒐊 has this value *pir*, whatever other values it may be found to have.

c 2

Line 20 furnishes us with an interesting variant. Text reads *ri-ib*, and as variant is given , thus showing that this character has this value also in addition to *kal, dan*, &c., which are other values shown to belong to it in another part of this Essay.

Line 22. According to IV R 70, column 4, line 22, the single variant  has the Assyrian rendering *alâku*, 'to go.' For the three underlined characters in the text we have the following syllabic values: 1st character=*id, it, iṭ;* 2nd sign=*ri, tal, dal;* 3rd sign=*la* (*see* Table of Values in any Assyrian Grammar). Remembering the useful rule, that the one syllable generally ends with the same letter as that with which the following begins, we read our text *it-tal-la*, and to this is to be joined the following character *ku*. So we have the verb *ittalaku*, which comparative Semitic Grammar teaches us to be the Ifteal form (reflexive) of the verb *alâku* (הלך), 'to go.' This reading shows us that the double  in the variant represents the Ifteal form of the verb, which IV R, plate 70, column 4, line 22, has shown us to be the value of the single character .

Line 24. In the text we have 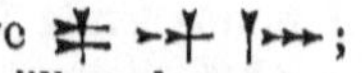; the variant gives as its equivalent 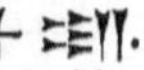. The characters in the text, according to II R, plate 2, No. 346 = 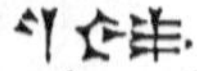. The variant reading has in common with this the value of *par-ṣu*. The variant reads *par-ṣi:* II R 2, 346=*par-ṣu*. *Par-ṣi* is plural of *parṣu*. The text gives us the plural sign, and leaves us then the two first characters to explain as above; their ideographic value, according to II R 2, 346, is *parṣu*, 'a command,' and here we are taught by the variant that this is the reading. Further on in this line we have as variant for 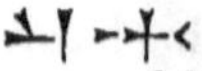 the character . The text reads *ḳa-ti*, the genitive case of *ḳatu*, 'hand,' the ideographic writing for which is represented by the variant. The reader will remember that I referred to this variant as illustrating the hieroglyphic character of Assyrian writing.

I have selected the above lines in order to show the great value of the variants, and also to show how they are to be used. A careful perusal of the page I have used will show the reader that there are also variants of minor importance, which only give a different form of the word to be read from that which the text suggests. Two examples will explain my meaning. The first two characters in line 25, according to the text=*na-dan*; the variant suggests *na-din*. Again, line 29, the text reads *pag-ri*; the variant suggests that we should read *pa-gar*, which is the construct state of the noun *pagru*, 'a corpse.' Here I close my remarks on the variants, the importance of which cannot be, I think, overestimated.

The Place of Assyrian among the Semitic Languages.

The Babylonian-Assyrian or Assyrian language is the language of the literature of the Cuneiform Inscriptions, with the exception of those that are in the Sumerian, Akkadian, and a few other languages. We shall here try to assign to Assyrian its proper place in the list of Semitic languages.

1. Assyrian. 2. Arabic [North and Middle]. 3. South Arabic. 4. Æthiopic-Amharic. 5. Hebrew. 6. Phœnician. 7. West Aramaic. 8. East Aramaic. It is possible to reduce this number to five by classing together those which are evidently related to one another. 7 and 8 go together, because they are both descendants of an older Aramaic language. 5 and 6 together = Canaanaic. These two have that relation the one to the other which the Biblical Aramaic has to the Syriac, and both can be referred to one original form. The one great difference between the two languages is that in Hebrew the substantive verb is הָיָה, whereas in Phœnician it is *kûn* (*cf.* the Arabic كَانَ = كَوَنَ). Again, 3 and 4 go together, for we know that the Æthiopians came from Jemen, in South Arabia. 1 and 2 remain distinct. Our list then resolves itself thus:—

1. Assyrian. 2. Arabic. 3. South Arabic. 4. Canaanaic. 5. Aramaic. Biblical tradition tells us that the Teraḥim went forth from Ur Kasdim to go into the Land of Canaan

(Genesis ii, 31). Hence it comes that the Canaanaic languages and the Assyrian have a large number of words in common with one another. The term אֲרָם is applied to those people settled in Syria, Mesopotamia, and the district extending to the upper plains of the Tigris. As in Canaanaic, so in Aramaic, there is a striking resemblance between the words in Syriac and Chaldee and those in Assyrian. The South Arabic, which includes Æthiopic, is more closely allied to Assyrian than its sister languages are, holding as it does a middle place between Assyrian and Arabic proper. But Assyrian cannot be classed under any of the other languages. It stands by itself, possessing more of the characteristics of the Old Semitic (Ur-Semitische-Sprache) than any of the cognate languages. On this ground, and also because it possesses a literature older than any other Semitic literature known to us, I have placed it at the head of this list of languages.

THE INFLUENCE OF ASSYRIAN ON HEBREW GRAMMAR AND LEXICOGRAPHY.

I.—On Hebrew Grammar.

§ 1. *The Relative Pronoun:*—The usual relative pronoun in Hebrew is אֲשֶׁר. How shall we explain this word? אֲשֶׁר is originally a noun, and according to the known laws in Semitic languages which govern sounds (*Lautgesetze*), is to be compared with أَثَر 'a place,' ܐܬܪ 'a place,' and አሠር 'a trace' (*vestigium*). In Assyrian *ašru* (אשר) is the usual word for 'place,' the construct state of which is *ašar*. *Cf.* *ašar talliki ittiki lullik*, *i.e.*, literally 'the place thou goest to, with thee will I go,' *i.e.*, 'whither thou goest will I go.' *Cf.* with this the Hebrew of Ruth i, 16. In the later books of the Old Testament we find alongside of אֲשֶׁר the form שֶׁ, with a daghesh in the following letter, *e.g.*, Judges v, 7; and before the guttural א we have שָׁ. Whence this שֶׁ? It is commonly said to be an abbreviation of אֲשֶׁר: but clearly this שָׁ or שׁ or שֶׁ is the Assyrian relative pronoun *ša*, the only one in the language. Certain are we that the relative pronoun is in the two proper names מְתוּשָׁאֵל and מִישָׁאֵל, where the שָׁ in the middle of the two words is in fact the relative pronoun.

§ 2. *The Prepositions:*—(*a.*) אֵת. This preposition is commonly derived from אֲנָת, which means 'meeting.' It is, however, clearly the same word as the Assyrian *it-ti*, which is the genitive case of *ittu*, 'the side, the border.' If this comparison with the Assyrian is accepted, the derivation of the word is different from the commonly accepted one. The plural of *ittu* is *itâti*, which could not be the plural if *ittu* =

intu: because if *ittu* were equal to *intu*, then the plural would be *inâti*, and not *itâti*. The root of the word must be אתה. אֵת means, therefore, 'by the side of,' 'together with.' This preposition is used in Assyrian with suffixes, as is the case with the Hebrew preposition. I append *itti*, with suffixes, in order that the student may compare them with the Hebrew:—

Singular	1st Person,			*it-ti-ia*,	i.e.,	*ittîa*, 'with me.'
	2nd	„	(mas.)	*it-ti-ka*,	„	'with thee.'
	2nd	„	(fem.)	*it-ti-ki*,	„	'with thee.'
	3rd	„	(mas.)	*it-ti-šu*	„	'with him.'
	3rd	„	(fem.)	*it-ti-ša*	„	'with her.'
Plural	1st	„		*it-ti-ni*	„	'with us.'
	2nd	„	(mas.)	*it-ti-ku-nu*	„	'with you.'
	2nd	„	(fem.)	*it-ti-ki-na*	„	'with you.'
	3rd	„	(mas.)	*it-ti-šu-nu*	„	'with them.'
	3rd	„	(fem.)	*it-ti-ši-na*	„	'with them.'

(*b*.) The accusative particle אוֹת (also אֶת) is the same as the late-Assyrian and late-Babylonian word *âtu*, as in the words *atûa*, 'what concerns me;' *atûni*, 'what concerns us.'

(*c*.) לְ, בְּ, כְּ. The etymology of these prepositions is very obscure. In Arabic we have *bi*, *li*, *ka* (the latter of which is really not a preposition); in Æthiopic we have *ba*, *la*; and in Syriac we have *bĕ*, *lĕ*; but the Assyrian has neither of these particles. Corresponding to בְּ it has *ina*, and to לְ *ana*. It has been supposed that the Assyrian preposition *la-pâni*, 'before,' was the same as the Hebrew לִפְנֵי, but this admits of some doubt. In the Assyrian *bašu*, 'in him'=בּוֹ, the *ba* is the same as בְּ, and *šu* is the 3rd personal pronoun suffix.

§ 3. *Adverbs.*—The ם-ending in adverbs is explained by the Assyrian. It is, in fact, the Assyrian indefinite pronoun *ma*. פִּתְאֹם 'suddenly'= Assyrian *pitîma*, and also *ina pitîma*; *mušâma*, from *mušu*, 'the night'=properly 'in the night, last night;' *šattišam* and *šattišâma*, from *šattu*, 'year'='yearly;' *pikâma*, from *pikû*, 'a moment'='momentarily.'

§ 4. *The Verb.* All the Semitic languages know only two tenses. Ewald, in his earlier writings, called them the 1st and 2nd Modus; later, Perfect and Imperfect. Böttcher calls them Perfect and Fiens. Nöldeke, in his Syriac Grammar, adheres to Perfect and Imperfect. We can keep the names Perfect (עבר) and Future (עתיד) in so far as we bear in mind (1) that the former expresses what is completed, the latter what is not completed; (2) that the Perfect and Future mark not merely the *Absolute* Past or Future in reference to the speaker, but also *relative* Past or Future in reference to another expressed action. The future אֶאֱהַב in itself, in connection with nothing preceding or coming after it = *amabo;* but in connection with other parts of the sentence, may mean *amo, amabam.* The Perfect אָהַבְתִּי in itself = *amavi,* but in connection with other parts of the sentence may mean *amaveram* and *amavero.* The existence of these two tenses derives support also from Assyrian, which has only the Imperfect and the Præsens (so named by Professor Delitzsch). In order to mark that something happens or will happen, or that one does something or will do something, the pure stems *ḳaṭal, ḳaṭul,* &c., were used; and to these were prefixed short pronominal stems, which referred either to the person who acted or the thing which happened, thus: *ja-ḳaṭal,* 'he kills;' *ta-ḳaṭal,* 'thou killest,' &c. The keeping of the full verbal stem expressed suitably the being-about-to-be. On the contrary, the stem was shortened as soon as a distinction had to be drawn between the completed and the incompleted, thus: from *jaḳaṭal,* the form *jaḳṭal* was used, and from *taḳaṭal,* the form *taḳṭal,* &c.

We find in the Imperfect sometimes the vowel *u,* sometimes *i,* sometimes *a.* The Assyrian also has preserved this old way of forming the Imperfect, for in it we have imperfects with each of these vowels: most commonly *u,* less commonly *i,* least commonly *a.* In place of *jaḳaṭal,* with its characteristic vowel *a,* the shorter form *jaḳṭul* (יִקְטֹל) came gradually into use. The form of the Imperfect with *a,* which had become superfluous, was then used in Hebrew to form the Passive;

but that the passive formation depends not on the vowel *a*, the Assyrian shows clearly. *Cf.* Assyrian *ju-ḳaṭṭal*, 'he kills many;' *juḳaṭṭil*, 'he killed many;' on the contrary, in Arabic and Hebrew, *juḳaṭṭil*, 'he kills many;' *juḳaṭṭal*, 'they were killed in large numbers.'

The old Semitic and the Assyrian have the power of expressing a circumstance as continuing, by joining the personal pronoun to the noun which expresses the action or quality. Thus, from *šarru*, 'a king,' we have a form, *šarraku*, 'I am a king'=*šarru*, 'king'+*anakû*, 'I;' *šarrata*, 'thou art a king'=*šarru*+*atta*, 'thou;' *gašraku*, 'I am brave'=*gašru*, 'brave'+*anakû*; *gašrâni*, 'we are brave'=*gašru*+*ani*. For these combinations compare I R, plate 17, line 32, where we read *šarraku*; *bêlaku*, 'I am lord;' *na'idaku*, 'I am exalted;' *gašraku*, &c. Exactly in this way was the simple verbal-stem *ḳaṭal* treated. Thus: *labiš*, 'he was or is clothed;' 3rd sing. fem. = *labšat*; 2nd sing. masc. = *labšâta*; 2nd sing. fem. = *labšâti*; 1st sing. com. = *labšâk(u)*; 3rd plur. masc. = *labšû(ni)*; 3rd plur. fem. = *labšâ(ni)*; 2nd plur. masc. = *labšatûnu*; 2nd plur. fem. = *labšatîna*; 1st plur. com. = *labšâni*.

The Imperative is *ḳĕṭôl*; with gutturals אֱמֹר and חֲמֹר, in verbs Intransitive or with medial signification, as שְׁכַב with final *a*. In Assyrian both syllables in the Imperative have the same vowel. Thus from *kašâdu*, 'to conquer,' we have *kušud*; so also *pikid* and *ṣabat*. This Imperative, with the same vowel in both syllables, is, I believe, the original Semitic form. כְּתֹב has as its ground-form *kutub*.

Verba Mediæ Geminatæ and Mediæ Vav or Yod.

1. *Verba Mediæ Geminatæ*.—These are in Assyrian always treated as strong verbs, and it is only in a few cases that we find additions for the purpose of assimilating the two last consonants. Thus *šalâlu* is conjugated *išlul*, *tašlul*, *tašlul*, *tašluli*, *ašlul*, &c. This is probably the oldest mode of treating these verbs, traces of which mode are to be found in the Hebrew. For examples, see Gesenius' Grammar, § 67, Remark 10.

The other mode of treating these verbs is by assimilating the two last consonants, and is of later origin. Thus the 3rd person Perfect can retain the two last like radicals, as *e.g.*, חָלַל and סָרַר; more frequently they are assimilated, as in דַּק and מַר. The Imperfect of the Niphal in one case has exactly the same form as that which strong verbs always have, viz. יִלָּבֵב, which is of the same form as יִקָּשֵׁל (Job, xi, 12).

2. *Verba Mediæ Vav and Yod.*—The roots of these verbs are generally treated as consisting of three radicals, but it is better to suppose with Nöldeke and August Müller (Z. D. M. G., xxiii, 698 *sq.*) that the roots consist of only two radicals, which are joined together by a vowel originally short, but made long through the law of three-consonantal roots. Thus, as the root of קוּם we take קָם. Assyrian favours and supports this mode of treating these verbs; 'he killed'=*i-dûk;* 'he stood up'=*i-ḳûm;* 'I turned back'= *a-tûr;* 'I subjugated'=*a-nir.* In the Imperative 'kill'=*dûk;* 'set fast'=*šîm.* It is only on the supposition of two-consonantal radicals that we can explain the participle active קָם, and such forms as קַמְתִּי, קַמְתְּ, קַמְתָּ. The middle letter *vav* owes its origin to the Imperfect form, where we have יָקוּם, and this ו in the Imperfect is of the same origin as the *u* in יִקְטֹל (original form *jaḳṭul*) (Gesenius' Grammar, translated by Davies, page 109).

II.—On Hebrew Lexicography.

It will not be uninteresting to the reader, I think, if I begin this part of my essay by bringing together Assyrian words with their Hebrew parallels:—

pû, 'the mouth' = פֶּה.

'aḫu 'the pot or vessel' = אָח or אַח, and by no means from אחח derivable.

idu, ‘the hand’ = יָד
dâmu ‘blood’ = דָּם
sûsu, ‘the moth’ = סָס
dâdu, ‘the beloved’ = דּוֹד
’îṣu, ‘wood’ = עֵץ
išâtu, ‘fire’ = אֵשׁ (Syr. = ܐܫܬܐ ‘fever,’ Æth. እሳት)
amtu, cstr. *am-at*, ‘the maid’ = אָמָה (አመት· ancilla)
bintu, cstr. *binat*, ‘the daughter’ = בַּת = בנת
daltu, pl. *dalâti*, ‘the door’ = דֶּלֶת
ḳaštu, pl. *ḳasâti*, ‘the bow’= קֶשֶׁת
šaptu, pl. *šapâti*, ‘the lip’ = שָׂפָה
’abu, ‘the father’ = אָב
’aḫû, ‘the brother’ = אָח
ummu, ‘the mother’ = אֵם. Root אמם. *Cf.* the Æthiopic.
ûmu, ‘the day’ = יוֹם (Aramaic יוֹמָא, Arabic يَوْمٌ)
šikaru, ‘wine’ = שֵׁכָר
agalu, ‘calf’ = עֵגֶל
libbu, ‘the heart’ = לֵב
šâru, ‘the storm, tempest’ = שְׂעָרָה
rêšu, ‘head’ = ראשׁ
šamšu, cstr. *šamaš*, ‘the sun’ = שֶׁמֶשׁ
irṣitu, ‘the earth = אֶרֶץ
lubultu (= *lubuštu*), cstr. *lubšat*, ‘clothing = לְבוּשׁ

בָּחוּר ‘the youth,’ plural בַּחוּרִים, has probably nothing to do with בָּחַר, ‘to choose out of a number,’ so that בַּחוּרִים should mean ‘the chosen ones.’ We may compare with it the Assyrian *baḫulu*, ‘the young man;’ plural *ba-ḫu-lâ-ti*, ‘the young warriors, male, and therefore warlike subjects.’ Sennacherib Inscription, I R, plate 37, column I, line 56, has *ba-ḫu-la-ti al Ḫi-rim-mê*, *i.e.*, “The warriors of the city Ḫirimmê.’

הֵיכָל, 'temple,' is not from יכל, 'to be capacious,' but is really a word borrowed from the Assyrian; *temple* in Assyrian = *ê-kallu*. This word is borrowed from the non-Semitic Akkadian *ê*, 'the house,' and *gal*, 'great;' so that *êkallu* means 'the great house,' hence 'temple, palace.' *Ekallu* is represented in Assyrian by two characters, 𒂍 𒃲, *i.e.*, 𒂍 + 𒃲. The first of these is the general ideograph for 'house,' and has the syllabic values *bît* (בַּיִת), *pît*, *ê*; *ê* is a value borrowed from the Akkadian word for 'house,' viz., *ê*, or with its consonantal ending *eš* (I refer the reader to Dr. Haupt's "Akkadische und Sumerische Keilschrifttexte," page 17, No. 266, where in the Akkadian we have *eš*, and in Assyrian *bi-i-tu*, i.e., *bîtu*). The character 𒃲 is the ideograph for *rabû*, 'great,' the equivalent of which in Akkadian is *gal*. The ideograph for *palace* then = *bîtu* + *rabû* = house + great; the Akkadian is *ê* + *gal*.

In Jeremiah l, 21, the enemies of Babylon are commanded to go up against הארץ מרתים and against the inhabitants of פקוד. The first name מרתים is explained in Gesenius thus: "Double obstinacy, or repeated rebellion, a symbolic name for Babylon." Ewald, in his last edition of "Die Propheten," translates it, "das land Doppeltroz," and then he properly adds "Aram-Naharaim, the land of the double-river, Mesopotamia." It is taken for granted by Ewald and the latest edition of Gesenius' Lexicon, that מְרָתַיִם is the right punctuation. The Assyrian shows that it is not. We know from the inscriptions of a land described as *mât marrâtim*. Now *marrâtu* means 'the sea,' so that '*mât marrâtim*' means 'the land of seas,' *i.e.*, South Babylonia. The word *marrâtu* occurs in the Inscription of Tiglathpileser II, II R 67, line 3. (*See* Appendix, Note 2.)

Again, פְּקוֹד Ewald explains as 'punishment,' the city Punishment, *i.e.*, Babylon. And this is also the explanation in Gesenius. But פְּקוֹד is no other than the famous warlike nomadic tribe *Puḳûdu* (*amêlu Puḳûdu*, in I R 37, 45).

In Ezekiel xxiii, 23, קוע and שוע have puzzled commentators. קוע is thus explained in the last edition of Gesenius. "According to the Hebrew commentators, Vulgate and others = Prince, Noble, properly stallion, breeding camel (which must be of noble breed), according to a transposition frequent in Arabic." שוע is rendered by *beatus*. Ewald, however, hits the mark when he says, "It is quite clear that the words פקוד ושוע וקוע cannot be anything else than proper names of smaller Chaldee peoples." We know now from the Inscriptions that *Su* and *Ḳu* were nomadic tribes in North and South Mesopotamia. I find in a Fragment marked M 55, in the British Museum Collection, which I copied at the beginning of last year, the following lines, viz., 12 and 13, Column 4:—

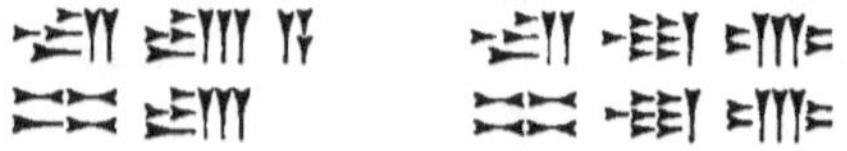

This part of the Tablet relates how the people on the sea-coast were at enmity with the people by the sea-coast—Subarta with Subarta, Assyrians with Assyrians, Elamites with Elamites, the Kaššû with the Kaššû, the *Sutu* with the *Sutu*, the *Ḳutu* with the *Ḳutu*, Lulubu with Lulubu, &c.; thus there was division among these peoples themselves. I quote this passage for the sake of the two names Sutu and Ḳutu, abbreviations of which were Su and Ḳu. Professor Delitzsch has, I think, clearly shown that these two peoples are the same as the שׁוֹעַ and קוֹעַ of Ezekiel. The student observes that the Hebrew has שׁ, while the Assyrian has ס. Further on, under the head of Biblical Geography, he will find that it often happens that the Assyrian ס corresponds to the Hebrew שׁ. The land *Su*, with the Determinative Suffix *ki*, for 'land,' is also mentioned in II R 23, 21*d*, 63*d*.

עַשְׁתֵּי is found in union with עָשָׂר, to denote 'eleven.' The student will find a note upon this word in the English edition of Gesenius' Grammar, p. 222. The explanation given by the translator in this note, viz., that עַשְׁתֵּי is a corruption of אֶחָד, is too far fetched. The only tenable explanation is that given by the Assyrian. *One* in Assyrian = *ištên*, which word itself is borrowed from the non-Semitic Akkadian *aš-tân*, which means 'one in number;' *ta-a-an*, *i.e.*, *tân*, not *tain*, means 'measure, number.'

חָרָן, in Assyrian *ḫarrânu*, means "the road along which traders pass, and on which they carry on their trade." It may be called the trade-road: it particularly refers to a point in the road where several persons meet to carry on their trade. The Akkadian word from which *ḫarrânu* is derived is *ḫarran*.

לוּן or לִין, 'to spend the night in a place,' is derived from לַיִל 'the night.' In Assyrian *lânu* = 'the court, fore-court of a house,' and the denominative verb *lânu* = "to bring into this court; to spend the night in the court under shelter of the house." I connect therefore the Hebrew with the Assyrian word *lânu*.

מְתִים occurs only in plural (Job xi, 3, Deut. ii, 34); it is constantly translated by Dillmann in his edition of Job ("Kurzgefasstes Exegetisches Handbuch zum Alten Testament'), 'die leute.' In Æthiopic we have this same word in singular, *met pl amtât*, 'maritus, vir.' In Assyrian the word for *maritus* is *mutu*, the ideograph for which is 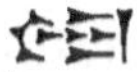, which character is also the ideograph for *aššatu*, 'wife.'

נָהַל and רָבַץ, in Psalm xxiii, 2, are synonyms like *na'âlu* and *rabaṣu* in Assyrian. In the simple Ḳal form these verbs mean 'to rest, to lie.' In the eighth edition of Gesenius there are brought together under נהל, the roots נהר, 'to flow;' נחל, 'brook, valley;" نَهِلَ, 'to drink for the first time, to drink to satiety (of the camel).' Then the steps are given by which the meaning 'to lead' is arrived at. Simpler far than this is the explanation by Delitzsch in Lotz's "Tiglathpileser I," p. 123, where he says, "נהל, 'to rest, encamp:' *Piel* = cause to rest, cause to encamp, give rest." In the Psalm, נִהֵל is parallel to הִרְבִּיץ, just as in Assyrian *na'âlu* is a synonym of *rabaṣu*; *cf.* 2 Chr., xxviii, 15, and xxxii, 12;

1 Chr., xxii, 18, where the rendering, 'to lead,' does not suit the passages, while that of 'to lie, to rest, to settle down,' gives a good sense.

צלמות. This word has been pointed (and is pointed in our Hebrew Bibles) צַלְמָוֶת, and translated, 'shadow of death,' from צֵל and מָוֶת. There can be no doubt that both this punctuation and translation are wrong. The verb *ṣalâmu* in Assyrian means 'to be dark,' and our noun is connected with this verb. We punctuate it צַלְמוּת, and translate 'darkness,' from a root צלם 'to be dark.' Worthy of notice are the remarks of Professor Franz Delitzsch, who says, "originally is צלמות no compound, but from a root צלם, ظلم, *opprimere, obtenebrare*, and means 'deep-darkness.'" (This I quote from the lectures which I heard.) It is further to be observed that צלמות in the Book of Job is constantly used among a number of words, all of which mean 'darkness,' but of various grades. Thus in Job x, 21, 22, we have four words meaning 'darkness,' viz., חֹשֶׁךְ, צַלְמוּת, עֵיפָה and אֹפֶל. *Cf.* further Job xii, 22, where 'darkness' suits the passage best. No competent critic now disputes this meaning.

תְּמוֹל and אֶתְמוֹל, 'yesterday;' in Assyrian the words corresponding to these are *timâli* and *itmâlî*, *itimâlî* and *ittimâli*.

מַלָּח occurs in Jonah and Ezekiel, and came late into use among the Hebrews. It is generally derived from מֶלַח, 'salt,' but this derivation is wrong. The Assyrian word for *sailor* is *malaḫu*, which is a word borrowed from the non-Semitic *malaḫ*, i.e., *ma*, 'the ship' + *laḫ*, 'to set in motion.' Hence *malaḫu* is 'the one who sets the ship in motion.' In Akkadian *malaḫ* = *ma* + *laḫ*; *ma* = the Assyrian *elippu*, 'a ship,' and *laḫ* = Assyrian *šalalu*, in the sense of *aliku*, 'to go.'

עוֹלָם, 'everlasting, eternity, age;' generally derived from עָלַם, 'to veil, hide.' With this root it has nothing to do.

Ewald is right when he says that it is a form like יוֹמָם, and that originally it was an adverb. In Assyrian 'everlasting' = *ûlu*. *Cf.* the phrases *ištu ûlu*, 'from everlasting;' *šá ul-tu ul-la*, i.e., *šá ultu ûla*, in the Babylonian text, referring to the temple of Ištar at Arbela. (See "Babylonian Texts," published by Mr. Pinches, page 17, line 2.) The student observes that if the root had a מ we should expect an *m* in the Assyrian word. Again, we have the phrase *ûm ûlûti*, 'the day of eternity;' and also consider well the form *ûlû-ma*, 'everlasting.' I would refer the reader to my remark on the ם-ending in adverbs, under the head "Hebrew Grammar," for an explanation of the ending *ma* in *ul-lu-ma*. (I R 59, col. 1. 41.)

אֶשֶׁד, as in Num. xxi, 15, וְאֶשֶׁד הַנְּחָלִים, does not mean, as in the authorised version, '*the stream* of the brooks,' but '*the bed* of the streams.' The word is not to be referred to the Syriac ܐܫܕ, 'fundere,' but it is best to compare it with the word *išdu* in Assyrian, which means 'foundation, base.'

לְבֵנָה, 'brick,' identical with the Assyrian *libittu* = *libintu*. *Tu* is the feminine ending in Assyrian, as ה ָ is in Hebrew. The verb *labânu* means 'to make bricks.'

פֶּחָה, plural פַּחוֹת. Schrader is right in regarding the word as Semitic, and it is undoubtedly not of Sanskrit origin (*see* Gesenius, last edition). The Assyrian word corresponding to it is *paḫâtu* or *piḫâtu*, which means 'satrapy,' as well as 'satrap:' 'province' in general, as well as 'governor of a province.'

כִּסֵּא, 'a throne,' corresponds to the Assyrian *kussu*, which is a word borrowed from the non-Semitic *guza*. The *g* in Sumerian changes to *k* in Assyrian, as in *engar*, which becomes *ikkaru*, 'the foundation.' So *guza* becomes *kussu*.

גָּמָל, 'the camel,' generally derived from جَمُلَ, 'to be beautiful, complete;' so that the camel, according to this derivation, is 'the beautiful, complete animal.' Better seems to me to be the derivation accepted by Assyriologists. In

Assyrian it is named *gammalu*, a non-Semitic word = *gam* + *mal*. *Gam* means 'a hump,' and *mal* 'to carry.' Hence the camel is the 'hump-bearing animal.'

תַּרְתָּן occurs in Isaiah xx, 2 Kings, xviii, 17; rightly explained in the last edition of Gesenius as the title of a high Assyrian officer. The Assyrian name is *tur-tan-nu*, and it is represented by two characters,  (whose syllabic value is *tur*, and ideographic value *mâru*, 'son') and  (whose syllabic value is *tan* or *dan*, and ideographic value *dannu*, 'mighty'), so that the Assyrian name means literally 'the mighty son,' *i.e.*, 'the officer in high position.' On the Canon of Eponyms marked C^b in Delitzsch's "Lesestücke," the title of the officer mentioned in page 94, line 28, is *amêlu tur-ta-nu*. Nebo-bel-uṣur was turtan of the city of Arpad. The title occurs several times in this same canon, viz., page 92, 9; page 93, 38, 48; page 94, 18.

טִפְסַר, Jeremiah li, 27, a word of Assyrian origin. The Assyrian word is *dupšarru*, 'the tablet writer,' represented in Assyrian by the characters ; the first character is a determinative meaning 'man,' *i.e.*, *amêlu*; the second character has the syllabic value *dup*, and the ideographic value *duppu*, 'a tablet;' the third character has the syllabic value *šar* or *sar*, and the ideographic value *šaṭâru* (שָׂטַר), 'to write.' The three characters then mean 'the tablet writer.' In the Akkadian language *dup* means tablet, and *šar* is the Akkadian equivalent of *šaṭaru*, 'to write.'

קָנֶה, 'reed,' generally derived from קָנָה, 'to stand upright;' so the last German edition of Gesenius. In Assyrian 'the reed' = *ḳanu*, the root of which is *gin* or *gan* in Akkadian, 'to bend;' the Akkadian for *reed* is *gi-en*, to be spoken *gên*. Hence the reed is called קָנֶה, because it bends, and not because it stands upright.

סוּס. The equivalent in Assyrian is *sisû*, which is the proper word for 'horse,' and not *murniski*, as has been long supposed.

מְאֹד, 'very,' originally means 'fulness, strength.' Professor Fleischer derives it from אוד, 'to oppress,' so that it means 'the burden.' In Assyrian we have the verb *mâ'du*, 'to be many,' and the noun *mû'du*, 'fulness, strength, multitude.' It seems to me best to connect the Hebrew word with the Assyrian.

כַּר, in Isaiah xxx, 23; Ps. xxxvii, 20, 65, 14, means 'meadow, park, plantation.' The Assyrian word is *kirû*, represented by ; the first character is the determinative for *iṣu* (עֵץ), 'wood,' and the second has the ideographic value *arḳu* (יָרָק), 'green:' so that the two characters together mean 'the green wood or park.'

יְאֹר, generally explained as a word taken from the Egyptian, inasmuch as it is always used for the Nile. I think, however, that it is a pure Semitic word. The poetic word for 'river, canal,' in Assyrian is *ja-u-ri;* and so יְאוֹרֵי means 'a river' in general. (IV R, plate 44, line 21.)

אִגֶּרֶת, explained in Gesenius as a Persian word, may be compared with the Assyrian *egirtu* or *igirtu*, the general word for 'a letter.'

קְדֵשָׁה. In II R 17, 116, the first word in this line is *ḳa-diš-tu*, which corresponds to the Hebrew word. The *tu* is the feminine ending, corresponding to the Hebrew ה ָ; in Hebrew, as in Assyrian, the consonants are the same, namely, קדש. It is interesting that in the very next line we should meet with the reading *iš-ta-rit*, corresponding to עַשְׁתֹּרֶת, *i.e.*, Astarte. In the hymn to the goddess Istar (K. 4, 931), obverse, line 12, we read, *um-mu ilu iš-ta-ri-tu*, *i.e.*, 'the mother of the goddess Astarte.' In the Sumerian hymn published by Haupt in his third part of the "Akkadische-Sumerische Keilschrifttexte," page 126, line 19, we read, *iš-ta-ri-tu ul ana-ku-ú*, *i.e.*, Astarte, not I. If we continue, we read in the same line, in the Assyrian, *mar-tu ḳa-dup-tu ilu, &c.* Is not *ḳaduptu* equal to *ḳadištu?* In this very line occurs (the first word) *ištaritu*, and from the fact that they occur together, we must, I think, read in this line *ḳadištu*, and not *ḳaduptu*. I express no opinion in regard to these words, but simply point out that they occur in these Inscriptions close to one another.

מָחוֹז, Ps. cvii, 30, translated 'sea-coast,' and by the old translators, 'haven, harbour;' in Assyrian *maḫâzu* is the usual word for 'place, village.'

רַבְשָׁקֵה, in Assyrian *rab-sak*, and represented by the characters 𒇽 𒃲 𒊕, *i.e.*, *amêlu*, *rabû*, *ḳaḳḳadu*, *i.e.*, 'man,' 'great,' 'head.' Hence the Rabshakeh was literally 'the chief of the great men.' In Land's "Syriaca Anecdota," Vol. III, page 259, line 8, we read of ܪܒ ܫܩܐ who was sent from ܣܢܚܪܒ. The word in Syriac means 'the lord of the legs or tribes.'

מָחָר, adverb and substantive = 'to-morrow.' Olshausen ("Grammar," § 38*c*) makes it = מאחר; generally derived from אחר, 'to be behind, remain behind.' The root מחר in Assyrian means 'to be in front, at the top, to be opposite.' So מָחָר is in Assyrian *ûmu pânu* and *ûmu maḫri*, 'the day in front.'

BIBLICAL GEOGRAPHY.

In this part of my Essay I propose to show what light Assyriology has been able to throw upon the Geography of the Bible. It will no doubt be interesting to students of Hebrew, to know how the names of places mentioned in the Bible are written in the Cuneiform Inscriptions, and to the student of history, to know on the Inscriptions of which kings of Assyria the places are mentioned. For a fuller account of some of the places than I shall give, I refer the reader to Delitzsch's work called "Wo lag das Paradies?" In the following pages I shall adopt the method of transcription now common among writers on Semitic subjects:—*s* = ס; *š* = ש; *ṣ* = צ; *ḫ* = ח; *t* = ת; *ṭ* = ט; *k* = כ; *ḳ* = ק; ' = א; ' = ע.

אֶרֶךְ, Gen. x, 10, is the Babylonian *Arku* or *Urku*, now the famous ruins of Warka, on the eastern bank of the Euphrates, between longitude 31° and 32° and latitude 43° and 44°. The Akkadian name of the place is Uruk (Ú-ru-uk), and is represented by the characters 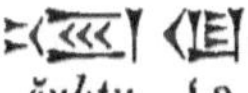, the first of which has the ideographic value of *šubtu*, 'a dwelling,' and the second being the usual determinative affix for 'land or place.' Uruk appears then to mean 'the dwelling,' κατ' ἐξοχήν. In Akkadian *ú-ru* is the equivalent of the Assyrian *šubtu*, and means 'dwelling.' In II R 50, 59–60*b*, the name is written *Ú-ru-uk*, *i.e.*, Erech.

אַכַּד, Gen. x, 10. This is a name we constantly meet in the Cuneiform Inscriptions, and it is generally represented by the character . The kings of Babylon are called 'the kings of Šumer and Akkad.' Akkad is no other than Agane, as the late George Smith conjectured, a part of the town Sippar, also called Sippar-Agade. Akkad is also the name for North Babylonia, as Šumer (Šu-me-ri, *i.e.*, שִׁנְעָר) is the name for South Babylonia. Šumer is represented by the characters , *i.e.*, 'the land *κατ' εξοχην*.' I refer the reader to a letter on the names Šumer and Akkad, which was written by Mr. Theo. G. Pinches, of the Assyrian Department of the British Museum, to the *Academy*, for July, 1882.

סְפַרְוַיִם, 2 Kings xvii, 24. Sippar and Agade form one town; the god of the former was Samas, the sun-god, and of the latter, the goddess Anunitu. Berosus names the town Sispara, Ptolemæus *Σιπφαρα*, and Plinius Hippareinum. Its Assyrian name is Si-ip-par, and is represented by the characters 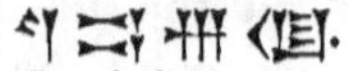. In connection with the name of this place, I might refer the reader to the above-mentioned texts edited by Dr. Haupt, Part II, p. 59, line 16. In the Assyrian column we read *ina ka-ri si-par*, and in the Akkadian column we read *kara* . . . . . *ta*, where we have in the space between *kara* and the ending *ta* the characters given above for the town of Sippara, and to these characters given on the Akkadian side correspond in Assyrian 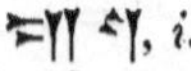, *i.e.*, Si-par. Its Sumerian name is Zimbir. Sippar is the present ruins of Aboo-habba, about 16 miles S.W. of Baghdad.

נִינְוֵה = Niniveh, the chief town of Assyria, the present Nebi-Junus and Kouyunjik. Its name on the Inscriptions is Ninâ or Ninua, of which Nina is the older name. The names occur too often on the Inscriptions to require special citation of passages where they occur. We find its name written thus, , *i.e.*, *ni-nu-a*, with the Determinative *ki*. Meaning of *ni* doubtful: *nu-a* = Assyr. *rabaṣu*, 'to encamp.'

אוּר, Gen. xi, 28–31; Nehemiah ix, 7, has אוּר כַּשְׂדִּים. Ewald sought this place in Armenia; but I think we shall not be wrong in saying that it is the famous Babylonian town Uru, now the ruins Mugheir, on the right bank of the Euphrates, south of Babylon. In II R 50, lines 44–47*b*, we have the name U-ri, which is our town Ur. The god of this town was the moon-god Sin.

אֶלָּסָר, Gen. xiv, 1, 9, is the Babylonian town Larsa. See II R 50, 48–49*b*, where we read the name La-ar-sa. Its oldest name was Ararzu. It is now the famous ruins of Senkereh, south-east of Warka. It is represented by the characters  (Samas, 'the sun-god'),  (*šubtu*, 'dwelling'),  (the determinative affix for 'town'), so that by these characters the town is designated as that in which the sun-god has his dwelling. (See V R 3, 107.)

כּוּת, 2 Kings xvii, 40, and כּוּתָה, 2 Kings, xvii, 24, a town east of Babylon, whose Babylonian name is Kutu, and Sumerian name Gûdûa. It is represented by the characters , *i.e.*, 'the place of prayer' (see II R 53, 4*a*). Kuthah often occurs on the Inscriptions in conjunction with Babylon and Sippar. The god of the town was Nergal (II R 60, 12*a*, *b*), with which agrees 2 Kings, xvii, 30.

בָּבֶל = Babylon; written in Assyrian sometimes syllabically thus: *ba-bi-lu*, and sometimes ideographically thus: 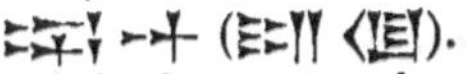. (See V R III, 107, and often.) The original name, therefore, was *Bâbilu*. According to the ideograph, the name means 'the gate of god.' The first character is the usual ideograph for *bâbu*, 'a gate;' the second character is the ideograph for *ilu*, 'god;' the third has the syllabic value *ra*, which is the Akkadian sign of the Dative Case. In Akkadian the word for *god* is *dingir*, and for *gate* is *kâ*, so that the ideograph is to be read *kâ-dingir-ra ki*. The oldest non-Semitic name of Babylon is represented by the characters whose syllabic values are *Tin*, *tir*, and *ki*. The first character, *tin*, has the ideographic value *balaṭu* (בלט), 'to live;' the second, *tir*, the value *kištu*, 'grove;' the third is the usual determinative affix for *town*. Hence 'Life-grove.'

כַּשְׂדִּים, generally connected with the name אוּר, are the Chaldeans. In the Cuneiform Inscriptions the name of Babylonia is *mât Kaldâ*, 'the land Chaldæa:' the Chaldeans are called *Kaldâ*. It is to be observed that the Assyrian name has *l*, while the Hebrew has *s*. This change of the original consonant *l* into *s* also occurs in the word *lubultu*, 'clothing,' for *lubuštu*, and *alṭur*, 'I wrote,' for *ašṭur*. The origin of the word is very obscure. The view of some scholars is that the word is derived from *kašâdu*, 'to conquer,' so that the *Kasdim* are 'the conquerors.' This derivation is, I think, a doubtful one.

אַשּׁוּר, the usual name for Assyria in the Old Testament, always denotes the kingdom of Assyria, and not the town. Its Cuneiform name is *Aššur*, and the name of its inhabitants is *Aššurâ*. The oldest name of Assyria is *Aušar*, which according to some means 'the watered meadows.' The name of the town is thus written:  or 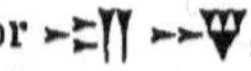, *i.e.*, *al ilu A-šur*, *i.e.*, 'city of the god Ašur;' and the name of the land thus: 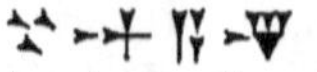 or 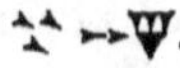. *i.e.*, *mât ilu A-šur*. In the Sumerian texts the name of the land is written , which is to be read *A-úšar*, according to Sᵇ, 146. This *úšar* = *ši-id-tum* (see Sᵇ, 146) = שָׂדֶה, 'meadow;' and  is the well-known ideograph for *mû*, 'water.' Hence, *A-úšar* has been explained as 'the watered meadows.'

חִדֶּקֶל = Tigris; in Assyrian *Diglat* and *Idiglat*, *i.e.*, *I-di-iq-lat*; represented by the characters 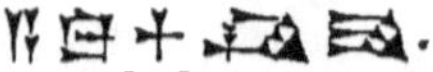. The first two characters are the usual ideograph for *nâru*, 'a stream or river;' and the remaining three, according to Sᵇ, 373, have the Assyrian value *šu-pu-ú*, which, together with *nâru*, is explained by Delitzsch as 'the stream which bursts forth, which rushes wildly on.' The Akkadian name is *I-di-ig-na*. For the Assyrian name, *cf.* II R 50, 7*c*, *d*.

פְּרָת = Euphrates; represented in Assyrian by the characters 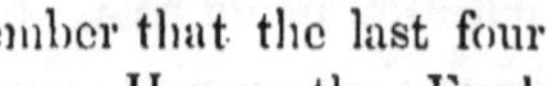, and = *Pu-rat-tu*. (See II R 50, 8*c*, *d*.) The two first characters = *nâru*, and the student will remember that the last four characters represent the town Sippar. Hence the Euphrates is designated by these characters as the River of Sippar or Sepharvaim. The Euphrates is also represented by the characters 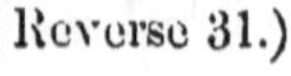, *i.e.*, 'the river of canals, the river from which the canals are fed.' The Akkadian name is *Puranunu*. (V R 22, Reverse 31.)

גּוֹזָן, 2 Kings xviii, 11; Isaiah xxxvii, 12. It is the neighbourhood into which the Israelitish exiles were taken. The river חָבוֹר is expressly named the Gozan in 2 Kings xviii, 11. The Assyrian name of the river is *Ḫâbûr*, and it is known by the same name up to the present day. In the Inscription of Assurnazirpal, I R, plate 18, line 77, "By help of Assur and Rimmon, the great gods who aggrandize my royalty, chariots and an army I collected: the banks of the Ḫâ-bûr I took." According to this inscription, the Chabor pours itself into the Euphrates not far from Carchemish. Gozan has the name Gu-za-na (II R 53, 54, and often). On the Canon History of Assyria, Rammânu-nirâri is said to have invaded Gu-za-na. It is the district watered by the Ḫâbûr.

רְחֹבֹת עִיר, Gen. x, 11. By עִיר Niniveh is to be understood: and the two words together form the name of the north-eastern part of Niniveh. In the Cuneiform Inscriptions it bears the name of Ribît Nina, *i.e.*, 'The broad squares of Niniveh.' (I R 45, col. 1, line 53, "ina ri-bît Nina *ki.*")

כֶּלַח, *in pausa* כָּלַח, Gen. x, 11, is the name of the southern part of Niniveh, and has in the Inscriptions the name *Kalḫu*. It is the present ruins of Nimroud, and is situated at the junction of the Upper Zab with the Tigris. It was built by Shalmaneser I, 1300 B.C., and raised into a residential town by Assurnazirpal (895–838 B.C.). The name is found in the Inscription of Assurnazirpal, I R, 17, line 9, where we read, *a-šib alu Kal-ḫi bêli râb-i bêli-a Aššur-nazir-pal šarru dannu, &c.*, "Dwelling in the city Kalḫu, a great lord, my lord, Assurnazirpal, mighty king, etc."

רֶצֶף, Isaiah xxxvii, 12; Cuneiform name=Raṣappa (II R 53, 37, where we read Ra-ṣa-ap-pa); present name=Ruṣâfa, a ruin in the Euphrates Valley. Reṣef and the other towns mentioned on this plate are towns in Mesopotamia.

בְּנֵי עֶדֶן, Isaiah xxxvii, 12, where it is mentioned along with Reṣef, Ḫaran, and Gozan; in Ezekiel xxvii, 23, along with Kalneh, Ḫaran, and Assur. The בְּנֵי עֶדֶן, we are told in Isaiah, dwelt in תְּלַ(א)שָּׂר, which was the name of the district between Edessa and Euphrates. This tribe bears the name Bît-Adini in the Inscriptions, *i.e.*, the tribe of which Adini was the founder. It was located between Ḫaran and Ktesiphon. Mentioned in Assurnazirpal Inscription, column 1, line 76, where we read, "Aḫîababa, son of Lamamana, whom they brought out of Bit-A-di-ni;" also in column 3, line 51. The tribe dwelt in the district of to-day which lies between Ainṭab and Urfa, on the left bank of the Euphrates. תְּלַ(א)שָּׂר =Tul-Ašurri, *i.e.*, Asurr's Hill, mentioned in the Esarhaddon Inscription, I R 45, column 2, 23, where we read, *mât Tul-A-šur-ri.*

אֲרָם, the land of the nomadic Aramæans, includes a part of Mesopotamia and that portion of land which stretches south-east towards the Persian Gulf. Cuneiform name is *Arâmu*, *Arûmu*, or *Arîmu*. *Cf.* the Nebi-Junus Inscription, I R 43, column 1, line 7, where we read, *amêlu A-ra-mi*, 'the people of Arâmu;' and III R, plate 8, line 38, where we read, *šar mât A-ru-mu.* In the Tablet of Tiglathpileser II, II R, plate 67, line 74, we have it written *mât A-ri-mê.*

חֵת, Gen. x, 15; that Syrian land which borders on its west side on Mesopotamia, and is separated from it by the Euphrates. Its Cuneiform name *Ḫatti* occurs frequently in the Inscriptions. Particularly interesting is the tablet in I R, plate 48, where are mentioned the twenty-two kings of Ḫat-ti ([cuneiform]) who were bound to pay tribute to the king of Assyria. The chief towns of Ḫatti are:—

כַּרְכְּמִישׁ, Isaiah x, 9, generally identified with *Κιρκήσιον*, *i.e.*, Circesium, a fortified town at the junction of the Ḫabor and Euphrates, on the right bank of the Euphrates, opposite Tulbarsip (whose present name is Biredjik, and whose Cuneiform name *Tul-bur-si-ip* occurs in the Monolith Inscriptions of Shalmaneser II, column 2, 14, III R, 7). *Gargamis* is its name in Assurnazirpal, column 3, lines 69 and 70; it is written *Gar* ([cuneiform]) - *ga* ([cuneiform]) - *mis* ([cuneiform]); but in the Inscription of Tiglathpileser I, column 5, line 49, its name is written *Kar-ga-miš.* Carchemish is represented to-day by the ruins of Ǵirbâs, on the right bank of the Euphrates.

אַרְפַּד, 2 Kings xviii, 34; Isaiah x, 9; Jeremiah xlix, 23, situated not far from Ḥamâth; its Cuneiform name is *Arpadda;* it is situated on the present uninhabited ruins Tel-Erfâd, about twelve miles north of Aleppo. Vulnirâri went up against the land Arpadda, 806 B.C. The name is also given in the Canon History, II R 52, 166, 30*b*, and often. (See further, Kiepert in Z. D. M. G., Vol. XXV, p. 655.)

חֲמָת, Num. xiii, 21; xxxiv, 8, a large Syrian royal city on the River Orontes; since the time of the Seleucidæ called Epiphania; named in Amos vi, 2 חֲמַת רַבָּה. Cuneiform name = *Ḫamattu* (II R 53, 37).

דַּמֶּשֶׂק, Damascus, a royal town on the River Chrysoras, named in the Inscriptions Dimašḳa (II R 53, fragment 4, line 56; and in fragment 3, line 68, and often). The second radical מ is never doubled in Assyrian. It has also another name, which marks it as the town of asses, viz., *ša imerišu: imeru* means 'an ass.' In Arabic its name is Dimašḳu.

כְּנַעַן includes in the Old Testament both Phœnicia and Palestine; this district in the Inscriptions, particularly the part bordering on the coast, bears the name *mat Aḫarri*, *i.e.*, the West Land. Canaan has the name *Gan-a-na* or *Kan-a-na.* Its chief towns are:—

צִידוֹן, Gen. x, 15; here spoken of as the first-born son of Canaan. The Cuneiform name of the town is *Ṣidûnu;* and in the Inscriptions we read of a great and small Ṣidon (Prism Inscription of Sennacherib, I R 37–42, column 2, line 38, where we read, *alu Ṣi-du-un-nu rab-u alu Ṣi-du-un-nu ṣiḫru*, *i.e.*, Ṣidôn the great, Ṣidôn the less). *Cf.* צִידוֹן רַבָּה, in Joshua xi, 8; also in I R 35, line 12, we read of a land *Ṣi-du-nu.* Its present name is Saïda.

צָרְפַת, 1 Kings xvii, 9, 10; Obadiah, 20 = Sarepta; Cuneiform name is *Ṣa-ri-ip-tu* (*Ṣariptu*), a Phœnician town lying between Tyre and Ṣidôn (Prism Inscription of Sennacherib, II, 39). From this inscription we gather that the Assyrian monarch began his famous march in the north and went southwards. Ṣariptu can then be no other than Sarepta, Zarpath (*see* Kiepert's Map of Palestine), which lies on the coast between Tyre and Ṣidôn. It is the little village of the present day called Ṣarfend.

צוֹר, Tyre; in the Inscriptions *Ṣur-ru* (*see* Shalmaneser II, Inscription in III R, plate 5, No. 6), where the people of Tyre are called *Ṣur-ra-a-a*, *i.e.*, Ṣurrâ. The name Ṣurru occurs in the Inscription No. 1 of plate 35*m* I R, line 12. *Cf.* also I R 48, Inscription of Esarhaddon, an inscription which is very important geographically, line 2, where we read, *mât Ṣur-ri*, *i.e.*, the land of Ṣurru (Tyre). Arabic name = صُور.

עַכּוֹ, now *'Akka;* Cuneiform name = *Akkû*. (Prism Inscription of Sennacherib, column 2, line 40, where we read *Ak-ku-ú*). Arabic name = عَكَّا.

חֹסָה, Joshua xix, 29; in Assyrian *U-šú-ú*, i.e., *Ušû*. (Prism Inscription of Sennacherib, II, 40.) It is a town in the tribe of Asher, and according to its position in the list of places mentioned in this inscription, must lie north of Achzib and south of Sarepta.

אַכְזִיב, Joshua xix, 29, is *Achzib*, a town lying between Tyre and Akko. Written in the Prism Inscription, 2, 40, *alu Ak-zi-bi*. Present name is *Ecdippa*.

עַרְקִי, Gen. x, 17, has been generally identified with *Arḳeh*, at the north-west foot of Lebanon, between Tripolis and Antaradus, one parasang from the sea (*see* the "Commentary of Kalisch," p. 272). It lies fifteen miles north of Tripolis, and is known to-day by the name of Irka. Its Cuneiform name is *Arḳâ* (mentioned in the Fragmentary Inscription of Tiglathpileser II, in III R 10, No. 2, line 2).

צְמָרִי, Gen. x, 18; about twenty-four miles south-east of Antaradus, near the river Eleutherus, and known by the name *Simyra*. Its Cuneiform name is *Ṣimirra* (mentioned in the same line as Arkâ, III R 10, No. 2, line 2; and also in Fragment 3 on the same page, line 35).

Palestine.

(*a*). The Kingdom of *Israel* has the Cuneiform name *Bit-Ḫumria*, or *Bit-Ḫumrî*, *i.e.*, 'the house of Omri;' also *mât Ḫumrî*, 'the land of Omri. In III R 10, No. 2, line 6, we read, *mât bit Ḫu-um-ri-a*. In the inscription from the palace of Bârkû-nirâri, I R 35, we read, line 12, *mât Ḫu-um-ri-i*. The other Cuneiform name of Israel is *Sir'al*, which occurs on the Monolith Inscription of Shalmaneser II, in III R (plates 7 and 8), plate 8, column 2, line 92, where the line begins, *mât Sir-'-la-a-a*, i.e., *mât Sir'lâ*, 'the land of the Israelites.' Its chief towns are:—

שֹׁמְרוֹן, in LXX Σαμαρεια, once written Σεμηρών (1 Kings xvi, 24). Its Cuneiform name is *Samerina* (II R 53, No. 4, line 1); and in Tiglathpileser II Inscription (II R 9, line 50) we read, "the city of the *Sa-me-ri-na-a-a*," *i.e.*, of the people of Samerina, *i.e.*, Samaria. Also the name *Šamsimuruna*, not *Usimuruna*. (*See* Prism Inscription of Sennacherib, column 2, 47, where we read, 'the city of the *Šam-si-mu-ru-na-a-a*.')

אֲפֵק, 1 Samuel xxix, 1; Cuneiform name = *Apḳu* (II R 53, 39*a*); it is the Aphek which lies north-west from Jezreel.

מְגִדּוֹ, also מְגִדּוֹן = Megiddo; in the south-west part of the plain of Esdraelon, and lying south-west of Aphek, the present ruins of Leǧǧûn (Legis). Its Cuneiform names are (1) *Magadû* (II R 53, Fragment 3, line 56, viz., *Ma-ga-du-u*), and (2) *Magidû* (II R 53, Fragment 4, line 58. viz., *Ma-gi-du-ú*).

(*b*). The Kingdom of *Judah*, יְהוּדָה, has the Cuneiform name *mât Ja-ú-di*. (*See* Nebi-Junus Inscription, I R 43, column 1, line 15; and often in the Inscriptions after the younger Tiglathpileser.) Its chief towns are:—

יְרוּשָׁלַיִם, *K'ri perpetuum* for יְרוּשָׁלֵם. Cuneiform name is *Ur-sa-li-im-mu*, i.e., *Ursalimmu* (Prism Inscription of Sennacherib, column 3, line 8). We have the same consonants in the Hebrew as in the Assyrian, except that שׁ takes the place of ס. This occurs often, and I mention it in order that the reader may gather for himself the examples which occur. The present name of Jerusalem is El-Kuds.

יָפוֹ or יָפוֹא, Ezra iii, 7; Jonah i, 3. Cuneiform name is *Ja-ap-pu-ú*, i.e., *Jappû* (Prism Inscription, column 2, line 66). Observe the long *u* at the end, corresponding to the Hebrew Khôlem; present name = Jāfa.

בֵּית דָּגוֹן, Joshua xv, 51 = Beth-Dagon. Cuneiform name = *Bit-Dagâna* (Prism Inscription, column 2, line 65). Lies south-east of Jāfa, *i.e.*, Joppa. This is not the Beth-Dagon mentioned in Joshua xix, 27, situated near Accho, in the tribe of Asher, but the town in Philistæa, situated on the road leading from Joppa to Jerusalem. This is evident from its place in the list of towns mentioned in the inscription. The reader observes that the meaning of the name of the place is "the house of the god Dagon." Observe, then, how the name of the god is given by the Assyrian scribe, thus, *Dagâna*. Present name is Bêt-Dedjān.

בְּנֵי בְרַק, Joshua xix, 45 = Benê-beraḳ, in the tribe of Dan, south-east of Joppa. Cuneiform name = *Ba-na-a-a-Bar-ḳa*, i.e., *Banâ-Barḳa* (Prism Inscription, column 2, line 66). Present name = Ibn-Ibraḳ.

לָכִישׁ, 2 Kings xviii, 14 = Lachish. Cuneiform name = *Lakisu*. Probably it is the present Umm-el-Lâkis, on the border of Philistæa, in the south-west corner of Judah, on the road from Gaza to Jerusalem. *Cf.* 1 R, plate 7, No. J.

אֶלְתְּקֵה and אֶלְתְּקֵא, Joshua xix, 44, xxi, 23; Cuneiform name = *Al-ta-ḳu* (Prism Inscription, II, line 76). It is a town which lay between Ekron and Timnah.

חָצוֹר, Joshua xv, 23 = Ḫazor; not the town in Naphtali nor in Benjamin, but one of the two in the tribe of Judah, and it must be sought for in the neighbourhood of Joppa. Assyrian name = *A-ṣu-ru* (Prism Inscription, column 2, line 66).

פְּלֶשֶׁת, *i.e.*, Philistæa, Gen. x, 14; Isaiah xiv, 29. Cuneiform name = *Palastu* or *Pilištu.* (*See* line 12 in I R 35, which I have before quoted, where we read at the end, *mât Pa-la-as-tu.*) We read in this line of the lands of *Ṣurru* (Tyre), *Sidûnu* (Ṣidôn), *Ḫumrî* (Omri), *Udûmu* (Edom), and *Palastu* (Philistæa). Also mentioned in II R 52. Observe line 40, where we read, *ša al Kal-ḫa a-na mât Pi-liš-tu.*

Its chief towns are:—

עֶקְרוֹן, Ekron, the most northerly of the Philistine towns. In the LXX it is Ἀκκαρών. Cuneiform name = *Am-ḳar-ru-na* (Prism Inscription, column 3, line 1; *cf.* also I R plate 48, line 5, where we read, *Itûṣu šar Am-Ḳar-ru-na*). The Assyrian form of the name, *Amḳarruna* = *Akḳarruna*, is to be compared with the Greek form. Present name = 'Âkir.'

אַשְׁדּוֹד, Ashdod; Cuneiform name = *Asdûdu* (Prism Inscription, column 2, line 51, where we read of the people *As-du-da-a-a*); also in line 7 of I R 48, we read of a king Nu-milku, of the city *As-du-di.* Present name = Esdûd. (Hebrew has שׁ and Assyrian ס.)

תִּמְנָה, Judges xiv, 19 = Timnah. Cuneiform names = *Tamnâ* (Prism Inscription, column 2, line 83) and *Tamanâ.* Lies south-east of Ekron and east of Ashdod. Present name = Tibne.

אַשְׁקְלוֹן, Ascalon; Cuneiform name = *Is-ḳa-al-lu-na*, i.e., *Isḳalûna* (Prism Inscription, column 2, lines 58 and 63). Also mentioned in I R 48, line 4, where we read of Mitinti, king of the city *Is-ḳa-lu-na.* On II R 67, line 61 (Inscription of Tiglathpileser II), the name is written *As-ḳa-lu-na.*

עַזָּה, Gaza; Cuneiform names = *Ḫazîtu* (Prism Inscription, column 3, line 26, we read *alu Ḫa-zi-ti*), *Ḫazzûtu*

(Tiglathpileser II Inscription in III R 10, No. 2, line 9, where we read *Ḫa-az-zu-tu*), and *Ḫazzûtu.* In I R 48, line 4, its name is *Ḫa-zî-tu* (*Ḫaziti* is genitive case). The Ayin in Hebrew is, as is well known, of two kinds, one corresponding to the Arabic ع ('Ain), the other corresponding to غ (Gain). The ע in עַזָּה corresponds to the Arabic غ. This is here represented by the Assyrian *ḫ*, *i.e.*, ח.

Before going on to the geography of Egypt, I shall add a promiscuous list of a few important places.

1. אֱדוֹם and אֱדֹם; in line 12, I R 35, the reader remembers the name *mât Ú-du-mu;* in the Prism Inscription, column 2, line 54, we read of a king Ârammu, king of the land of the *U-du-um-ma-a-a*, *i.e.*, of the people of Udûmu.

אַרְוַד = Arvad; Cuneiform name = *A-ru-da* (Prism Inscription, column 2, line 49). The inscription does not help us to decide where Arvad was situated. (See Delitzsch's "Paradies," p. 281.)

עַמּוֹן, or more frequently בְּנֵי עַמּוֹן. Cuneiform name = *Bît-Ammânu* (Prism Inscription, column 2, line 52, has *Bît-Am-ma-na-a-a*, where Ammânâ denotes the people of the tribe of which Ammon was the founder). In V R, column 7, line 110, we read of a city *Bît-Am-ma-ni*, where Ammâni is genitive case after Bît.

מוֹאָב, Moab; Cuneiform names = *Ma'bu*, *Mâbu*, and *Mu'âbu.* Prism Inscription has *mât Ma'-ba-a-a*, *i.e.*, the land of the people of Ma'bu. In V R, column 7, line 112, its name is *Mu'-â-ba.* It is to be observed that in Assyrian as in Hebrew the middle radical is a guttural.

Egypt.

The Semitic name of Egypt is מִצְרַיִם, مِصْرَيْن. Nowhere in the Egyptian monuments does this name occur. As to the various ways of explaining this word, I refer the reader to Gesenius's Dictionary, or any other large Hebrew lexicon.

In the narrower sense of the word מִצְרַיִם is Lower Egypt. In the Inscriptions the corresponding name is *Mu-ṣur* (*see* V R, Annals of Assurbanipal, column 1, line 59, and often). In the two-lined inscription No. 4, in I R 48, we read as follows:—

mât Aššur-aḫ-iddina šar kiššâti šar mât Aššur
mâ-ti Mu-ṣur mati Ku-si

i.e., land of Esarhaddon, king of multitudes, king of Assyria, of the land Muṣur, of the land Kusu.

The name also occurs in No. 5, line 4, at the end. Muṣur is the name given to Lower Egypt. Its later Cuneiform name is Miṣir. Arabic name is Miṣr.

פַּתְרוֹס, Isaiah xi, 11; Jeremiah xliv, 15, is the name for Upper Egypt. In Isaiah xi, 11, we have the three names Miṣraim, Pathrôs, and Kush together. Pathros in old Egyptian is *pe-to-rês*, *i.e.*, the land of the South (so Professor Franz Delitzsch in his "Commentary"). In I R 48, No. 5, lines 4 and 5, we read, *šarrâni mât Mu-ṣur mât Pa-tu-*[*ru*]*-si mât Ku-si*, *i.e.*, "kings of the land Muṣur, of the land of Paturusu (Pathros), of the land of Kusu" (כּוּשׁ). Here the Assyrian and the Hebrew have ס in the name of Pathros.

כּוּשׁ, Æthiopia. Muṣur is in the north, south of it is Pathros, and south of Pathros is Kush. Cuneiform name = *Kusu* (*see* on פַּתְרוֹס; also in V R, column 1, line 67, and often). The Babylonians name it Kûšu, *i.e.*, the dark-coloured race, from *kuša*, the Assyrian for 'black.'

The chief towns of Egypt are:—

צֹעַן, Num. xiii, 22; Isaiah xix, 11; Ps. lxxviii, 12, 43 = Tanis. It has two names in the Cuneiform Inscriptions. (1) *Ṣi'nu* (a guttural as middle radical), *see* Assurbanipal, V R, column 1, line 91. (2) *Ṣa'nu* (ditto, column 1, 96). It lies between the *Ostium Sebennyticum* and the *Ostium Pelusiacum* of the Nile.

אוֹן, Gen. xli, 50, the well-known city of the Sun, with the Greek name Heliopolis; the city On, situated a few miles north of Memphis, called by Assurbanipal *Ûnu*.

מֹף, Hosea ix, 6; in Isaiah xix, 3; Jeremiah iii, 6, נֹף = מֶנֹף = Memphis; on the western bank of the Nile, south of Cairo. Present name among the Copts is Menfi. Cuneiform name = *Mempi* (Assurbanipal, V R, column 1, lines 60, 90, and often), *i.e.*, Mê-im-pi or Mi-im-pi. Arab. = منف.

נֹא, Ezekiel xxx, 14, 16, and נֹא אָמוֹן, Nahum iii, 8, is the old town of Teben or Thebes. Cuneiform name = *Ni'u* (Assurbanipal, V R I, 88, line 109, and often). In this inscription we are told that the king Tirḫakah, who was in Memphis, heard of the defeat of his army, abandoned the city, and fled into Thebes (*Ni-'*). The first character = *ni*, and the second character is the usual one for a guttural.

פוט. third son of Ham; his descendants are named along with Kush and Miṣraim in Nahum iii, 9. The Egyptologists identify Pût with Punt: according to Ebers, Arabic nomadic tribes tributary to Egypt. On the Darius Inscription of Nakshi Rustam, along with Kuš is mentioned a people *Pu-u-ta*, *i.e.*, Pûta, and probably the same as *Put* in Nahum.

There still remain a few names to which I wish to draw the reader's attention. They are the following:—

עֵילָם = Elam = Susiana, and in Gen. x, 22, mentioned as the first son of Shem. Its Cuneiform name is *Elamtu*, mostly written ideographically, and sometimes syllabically (thus, *ê-lam-tu*). It is generally represented by the characters 𒉏 𒈠 𒆠, and from these it is clear that the name means *highland*. The first character is the ideograph for *êlamu*, 'high;' and the third for *irṣitu* (ארץ), 'land;' the second has the syllabic value *ma*. Its Akkadian name is Êlama. Its chief town is שׁוּשַׁן, Nehemiah, i, 1, Daniel, viii, 2; Cuneiform name = *Šušân*. (*See* Assurbanipal, V R, column 7, line 1.)

לוּד, mentioned as the fourth son of Shem = the Lydians. Cuneiform name *Lûddu*. In V R, column 2, line 95, we read of Gyges, king of the land of *Lu-ud-di*.

עוּץ, Job, i, 1, lies north-east of Edom, in North Arabia, perhaps in the wilderness of Arabia, east of Palestine. Its Cuneiform name = *Uzzu*.

אֲרָרַט, a province of Armenia (2 Kings xix, 37), identified with Hara-haraithi, 'the mountain of mountains.' In the Babylonian Inscriptions its oldest name is Urašṭu; among the Assyrians it was called Urarṭu (*see* V R, x, 40, where the line reads, 'Saduri, king of the land Ur-ar-ṭi,' *i.e.*, Ararat). On the Bronze Gates of Shalmaneser II, discovered by Mr. Rassam at Balawat, column 3, line 3, we read of the land U-ra-ar-ṭi. (*See* the paper by Mr. Pinches in the "Transactions of the Society of Biblical Archæology," Vol. VII, Part 1, 1880.)

פָּרַס = Persia, Persians; Cuneiform name = *Parsu.* In the account of the capture of Babylon by Cyrus, obverse, column 2, line 15, we read of Cyrus, king of the land Par-su. In I R, 35, a plate I have often referred to in this geography, line 8, we read the names of several lands, viz., Mu-un-na, *Par-su-a*, Al-lab-ri-a, Ab-da-da-na. The word Parsua is here in accusative case, governed by a verb meaning 'to conquer, to take possession of.' Parsu-a = Persia. Arabic = فُرْس.

מִנִּי, Jeremiah, li, 27, a province of Armenia; Cuneiform name = *Mannu.* In the Historical Canon, II R, 53, we read, *ana mât Man-na-a-a*, "to the land of the Mannu people;" as also in the same canon, *ana Mad-a-a*, "to the Medes." The pointing of מדי in Hebrew is מָדַי; may not מני have been pointed at some time or other in the same way?

Here I close the list, and the reader desirous of further information, I would refer to the works of Schrader, "Die Keilinschriften und das alte Testament," 2nd edition, 1883, a translation of which into English is now in course of preparation; and Delitzsch, "Wo lag das Paradies?"

BIBLICAL HISTORY.

References to the Kings of Israel and Judah in the Inscriptions:—

1st.—Kings of Israel.

(*a*). Omri, whose Assyrian name is *Ḫumrî* (Hebrew = עָמְרִי), is mentioned in the Inscription of Shalmaneser II (858–823 B.C.), in his account of his victory over Hazael (Assyrian name = *Ḫa-za-'-ilu*, and Hebrew = חֲזָאֵל, 2 Kings viii, 15) of Damascus. *See* III R 5, No. 6, where we read at the close of this little inscription, the first discovery of the late George Smith, *madâtu ša mât Ṣur-ra-a-a mât Ṣi-du-na-a-a ša* ꜱ *Ja-ú-a apil Ḫu-um-ri-i am-ḫar, i.e.*, "the tribute of the land of the Tyrians, of the land of the Ṣidonians, of Jehu son of Omri, I received." The reader will also remember that Israel is called by the Assyrians *mât Ḫumrî*, 'the land of Omri.' (*See* Geography.) Observe that the Hebrew ע is represented in Assyrian by *ḫ* in Omri's name.

(*b*). Ahab: Hebrew אַחְאָב, *i.e.*, 'brother of the father;' Cuneiform name is *Aḫabbu*, mentioned in the Inscription of Shalmaneser II, III R, plate 8, column 2, line 91, where we read as follows: *Ša imêri-šu* 700 *narkabâti* 700 *bit-ḫal-lu* 10,000 *ṣâbî ša Ir-ḫu-li-ê ni mât A-mat-a-a* 2,000 *narkabâti* 10,000 *ṣâbî ša A-ḫâ-ab-bu, i.e.*, "of Damascus; 700 chariots, 700 magazines, 10,000 men of (= belonging to) Irchulên of Hamath, 2.000 chariots, 10,000 men of (= belonging to) Ahab." Ahab is here named in connection with the battle of Ḳarḳara (854 B.C.), where there were twelve Syro-Phœnician kings engaged against Shalmaneser, one of whom was Ahab.

(c) Jehu = יֵהוּא; Cuneiform name = *Ja-ú-a;* mentioned along with Hazael of Damascus in the passage cited about Omri. The inscription relates how Shalmaneser, in the eighteenth year of his reign, 840 B.C., crossed the Euphrates, defeated Hazael, captured 16,000 warriors, together with their weapons, took 1,221 war-chariots, shut Hazael up in Damascus, destroyed his parks, marched as far as the mountains of the land of Ḫaurân, and laid waste cities without number. And last of all he speaks of the tribute which the people of Tyre and Sidon and Jehu paid him.

(*d*). Menahem = מְנַחֵם, 2 Kings xv, 17–23; Cuneiform name is *Meniḫimmu;* mentioned in the 3rd fragment of Tiglathpileser II (III R 9, line 50), where we read his name thus: *Mé-ni-ḫi-(im)-mé al Sa-me-ri-na-a-a*, *i.e.*, "Menahem of the city of the people of Samerina," *i.e.*, Samaria. Mr. Rodwell's translation in the "Records of the Past," Vol. V, page 48, line 2, does not help the reader to see that 'Samirinai' is Samaria. The *a-a* at the end of the proper nouns always denotes the *people* of the city to whose name these letters are added. Menahem is also mentioned on the famous Prism Inscription of Sennacherib, column 2, line 47, as *Me-in-ḫi-im-me Šam-si-mu-ra-na-a-a*, *i.e.*, "Mênḫimmê of Samaria." He here appears as a vassal of Sennacherib.

(*e*). Peḳaḥ = פֶּקַח: Cuneiform name = *Pa-ḳa-ḫu* (the same consonants as in Hebrew, viz., פקח); mentioned by Tiglathpileser II (III R 10, fragment 2, line 28). Tiglathpileser came into the land of Peḳaḥ, conquered the northern districts of Israel, took their inhabitants away to Assyria, and Hoshea "he appointed over them." In 2 Kings xv, 29, Tiglathpileser is named as king of Assyria; while in v, 19, Pul is named as the king. Both names refer to the same person, for there was no other king of Assyria at this time but Tiglathpileser II (745–727 B.C.).

(*f*). Hošea = הוֹשֵׁעַ, 2 Kings xv, 30, whose Cuneiform name is *Ausi'*, is also mentioned by Tiglathpileser II (III R 10, fragment 2, line 28), where we read, *Ausi' ana šarrûti ana êli-šu-nu aš-kun*, *i.e.*, "Hoshea to the kingdom over them I appointed." "Ten talents of gold, one thousand of silver, I received from them" (the people) "as their tribute, and to the land of Assyria I sent." In Assyrian this name is written with ס; in Hebrew with שׁ.

2nd.—Kings of Judah.

(*a*). Azariah, 2 Kings xv, 2 = עֲזַרְיָה; in 2 Chron. xxii, 6 עֲזַרְיָהוּ. Cuneiform name = *Azrijaú:* is also mentioned by Tiglathpileser II, who made war against Azariah about 739 B.C. The Inscription, viz., III R, page 9, No. 2, is very much broken, so that no continuous extract can be given. Line 4 reads, *Aš-ri-ja-u mât Ja-u-di ina*, &c., *i.e.*, "Azariah, king of Judah in, &c.;" in fragment 3, line 9, in the same page, his name reads *Az-ri-a-a-ú*. The biblical date of this king is 808–757 B.C., which clashes with the date we should take from the Inscriptions.

(*b*). Ahaz, 2 Kings xvi, 2 = אָחָז (biblical date is 742–727 B.C.). Cuneiform name = *Jauḫazu;* also mentioned by Tiglathpileser II, after 731 B.C. *See* II R 67, line 61, where we read *Ja-u-ḫa-zi mât Ja-ú-da-a-a*.

(*c*). Manasseh, 2 Kings xxi, 2 Chron. xxxiii = מְנַשֶּׁה; mentioned in the Annals of Esarhaddon and in the Annals of Assurbanipal under the name *Menase*. In the Annals of Esarhaddon, III R 16, column v, lines 12, 13, we read, *ad-ki-ê-ma šarrâni mât Ḫat-ti u ê-bir tihamti Ba-'a-lu šar mât Ṣur-ri Mê-na-si-ê šar al Ja-ú-di*, *i.e.*, "I assembled the kings of Syria and (of the lands) beyond the sea, Baal king of Tyre, Manasseh king of Judah." These two lines are also the first two lines in the important Inscription I R 48, No. 1. *Menase* is here a vassal of the Assyrian king. As in many other proper names, we have here again the Samech in Assyrian for the Hebrew Shin.

(*d*). Hezekiah = חִזְקִיָּה and חִזְקִיָּהוּ. Cuneiform name is *Ḫazaḳijaú:* mentioned in the Prism Inscription of Sennacherib, column 2, line 71, where we read, *a-na Ḫa-za-ḳi-ja-ú mât*

Ja-ú-da-a-a, i.e., "to Hezekiah, king of the land of Judah." In column 3, lines 11 and 29, his name is written *Ḫa-zi-ki-a-ú*. The following is briefly the *Biblical account* of the war between Sennacherib and Hezekiah, 2 Kings xviii, 3, 19 *sqq.*: Sennacherib came up against all the fenced cities of Judah and took them. Hezekiah sends to Sennacherib to Lachish, with the prayer that he should withdraw on the payment of a tribute. Sennacherib agrees to this; receives 300 talents of silver and 30 talents of gold, all the silver in Jahveh's house, and the king's house: yet he withdraws not. He sends three officers, viz., the Tartan, Rabshakeh, and the Rabsaris, to Hezekiah to make certain proposals. They return to find their lord at Lachish, but on the point of besieging Libnah. Tirḫaḳah, king of Æthiopia, comes out against Sennacherib; Sennacherib shall not enter Jerusalem nor shoot an arrow into the city.

The Inscription Account.—Sennacherib tells us: On his third compaign in 701 B.C., he marched towards the Western Land, conquered the Phœnician towns, subdued Ascalon and advanced against Eḳron. The Eḳronites had dethroned and chained their king Padiah, who was on his way to Assyria, and then had gone over to Hezekiah, king of Judah. The princes and people of Eḳron gave over Padiah to Hezekiah. They did their dark deed with a feeling of hostility towards Assyria; and afterwards the recollection of what they had done caused them to fear. The kings of Egypt and of Æthiopia, with their forces, came to aid the people of Eḳron against Assyria, and within sight of the town of Eltekeh the decisive battle was fought. "With the help of Aššur my lord," says Sennacherib, "with them I fought, and caused their overthrow." The chief men belonging to Egypt and Æthiopia are taken alive in the midst of the battle. Eltekeh and Timnah are besieged and taken, and their spoils carried away. He moves northwards towards Eḳron, puts to death the princes and chief priests who had handed over the faithful Padiah in chains to Hezekiah. Their bodies are suspended on stakes round the city. He counts as spoil the people who had rebelled against him, and those who had not rebelled he commanded to be spared. Padiah is taken out of Jerusalem, whither he had been brought when handed over by the rebel princes to Hezekiah, and is set again on his former throne. Hezekiah, who had assisted the rebels, Sennacherib now proceeds to punish. The king of Judah ought not to have received as prisoner a king who was faithful to Assyria, who was "lord of the agreement and the oath of Assyria;" he had not submitted to the yoke of Sennacherib, and so the Assyrian monarch takes from the king of Judah forty-six of his strong cities, castles, smaller towns without number, 200,150 people, small and great, male and female; horses, bullocks, asses, camels, oxen, sheep without number, he carries away to Assyria. Hezekiah himself he shuts up "like a bird in a cage" in Jerusalem, his royal city. He binds towers round about the city, and blocks up the great gate so that the besieged cannot escape. The ruined cities he hands over to Mitinti, king of Ashdod, Padiah, king of Eķron, and Ṣilli-bêl, king of Gaza, who were faithful in their allegiance to him. Hezekiah is overwhelmed with the fearful splendour of the majesty of Sennacherib. The workmen and the coloured soldiers whom he had brought into Jerusalem to fortify it he now orders to carry tribute into Nineveh, the Assyrian royal city, viz., 30 talents of gold and 800 talents of silver, glass . . . . . . large precious stones, couches of ivory, fixed thrones of ivory, skins of elephants, teeth of elephants, *êšu* wood, *ku* wood (each of these in abundance), his daughter, the women of his palace, the *nâre* and *narâti* (some scholars explain these as the male and female musicians, but as I doubt the correctness of this explanation, I leave the words untranslated); and to do homage to Sennacherib he sends his envoy.

Let us compare these two accounts: Sennacherib tells us why he went up against Hezekiah, viz.. because he had received in chains of iron the faithful Padiah, king of Eķron, from his rebellious subjects. There is no mention of this in the Bible. There is also no mention of the town of Lachish in the Inscription account. The tribute was sent to Lachish according to the Bible, and according to the Inscription to

Nineveh. The non-mention of Lachish by the Assyrian scribe is, as Mr. Fox-Talbot explains, an omission arising from the brevity of the Assyrian narrative.

The Biblical account speaks of 30 talents of gold and 300 talents of silver; the Inscription of 30 of gold and 800 of silver. Fox-Talbot regards this as "an error in the manuscripts." It is, however, unnecessary to suppose that there is an error here at all. Brandis, in his work called "Das Münzmass- und Gewichts-wesen in Vorderasien bis auf Alexander den Grossen," Berlin, 1866, says, in page 101, that the Assyrian silver talent weighed 16·830 kilogrammes; on page 103 he says that the Hebrew silver talent weighed 43·650. Thus the silver talents of the two countries stood to one another in the proportion of 8 to 3. This, then, reconciles the seeming contradiction of the two accounts. On page 98 of this same work he writes: "The comparison of the two accounts" [the one in the Bible and the one given by Sennacherib*] "is in the highest degree interesting, inasmuch as it shows that the Hebrews reckoned according to the Assyrian *gold* talent, but according to a different silver talent, which stood to the Assyrian in the proportion of 8 to 3."

Tirḫaḳah, mentioned in the Biblical account, is the third king of the XXVth dynasty. Sennacherib speaks of him in his Annals, and his name, Tarḳu, frequently occurs in the Annals of Assurbanipal. *Cf.* V R, column 1, line 53, where we read, Tar-ḳu, king of Muṣur and Kusu. *See* also lines 78, 83, and often.

Nebuchadnezzar and his Successors.

Nebuchadnezzar. This name is written in two ways in the Bible, viz.: (1) נְבוּכַדְרֶאצַּר (Jeremiah xxi, 2, and often), which corresponds to the Babylonian mode of writing the name, viz., *Nabû-kudurri-uṣur*. (2) נְבוּכַדְנֶאצַּר (2 Kings xxiv, 1, and often). The Babylonian name shows that they knew the name with a *Resh* after the Daleth, and not with a Nun.

* These words in brackets are inserted by me.

In I R, plate 65, his name is written in full, *Na-bi-um-ku-du-ur-ri-ú-ṣu-ur*, *i.e.*, "Nebo, protect the landmark." *Nabû* is the god Nebo; *kudurru* = 'a landmark;' *uṣur* is the Imperative Mood of *naṣâru*, 'to protect.' In a new fragment of Nebuchadnezzar III, written in the Babylonian character, and published by Mr. Pinches in the "Transactions of the Society of Biblical Archæology," Vol. VII, Part 2, 1881, we find on the obverse side, line 13, written ideographically, *Nabû-kudurri-uṣur.* According to the Egibi Tablets his date is 604–561 B.C.

אֱוִיל מְרֹדַךְ, Evil-Merodach (2 Kings xxv, 27); first known on the Inscriptions through the Egibi Tablets, which the late George Smith purchased at Baghdad. He was the only son and successor of Nebuchadnezzar, and has the Babylonian name *Amêl-Marduk*, *i.e.*, Merodach's man. Merodach is the well-known Babylonian god Marduk. The date of this king is 561–558 B.C.

נֵרְגַל שַׁרְאֶצֶר, Jeremiah xxxix, 3 = *Nergalšarezer*, son of *Bêl-šum-iškun*, and son-in-law of Nebuchadnezzar. His name in I R, plate 67, line 1, reads *Nergal-šar-ú-ṣu-ur šar Bâbîli*, *i.e.*, *Nergal-šar-uṣur*, king of Babylon. His name means 'Nergal, protect the king.' His date is 558–554 B.C.

Nabunaid, *i.e.*, 'Nebo is exalted' (*naidu* = Arab. نَيِّدٌ). In I R, plate 68, column 2, line 19, we read, *ja-(a)-ti Nabu-naid šâr mât Bâbîli*, *i.e.*, "myself, Nabunaid, king of Babylon." Under his rule, 544–537 B.C., Babylon was conquered. Daniel, chapter 5, tells us that Babylon was conquered under King Belshazzar. In this same inscription, lines 24–26, we read, *u ša Belu-šar-uṣur aplu riš-tu-ú ṣi-it lib-bi-ia*, *i.e.*, "and of Belshazzar, my eldest son, the offspring of my body." The words, "the son of the king," are constantly used in the annals written in the time of Cyrus. Belshazzar was commander of the army in Akkad. Josephus speaks of Belshazzar "whom the Babylonians called Nabonidus." It seems certain, therefore, that Belshazzar never reigned, and that his name only appears in the Bible because the Jews confounded him with his father. (*See* Josephus, "Antiquities," Book 10, chapter xi, § 2.) We read in the inscription containing an account of the capture of Babylon by Cyrus, published by Mr. Pinches in the "Transactions of the Society of Biblical Archæology," Vol. VI, Part 1, 1880, "The seventh year the king was in Tevā; the son of the king, the great men and his soldiers (were) in Akkad, &c." Often on this inscription occurs the words *apil šarri*, 'the son of the king.' Though Belshazzar, son of Nabonidus, is not once mentioned by name, it is evidently he who is meant when the 'son of the king,' who was with the army in Akkad, is spoken of.

כֹּרֶשׁ, Ezra i, (538–529 B.C.) = Cyrus; Cuneiform names = *Kuras*, *Kurrašu*, *Kuršu*, &c. On a terra-cotta cylinder of Cyrus, brought by Mr. Rassam from the excavations at Babylon, we have the genealogy of the great king, and an account of the capture of Babylon by him. On lines 20 and 21 the genealogy of Cyrus is given, and here the name is written *Ku-ra-aš*. On the first line of the obverse of the inscription his name is *Ku-raš*.

דָּרְיָוֶשׁ = Darius, son of Hystaspes (Ezra iv, 5; Haggai i; Zechar. i, 1); Cuneiform names = *Da-ri-ia-mus*, *Da-ri-ia-uš*, *Da-ri-mu-šu*, &c.

אֲחַשְׁוֵרוֹשׁ, Ahasuerus, of the Book of Esther, generally identified with Xerxes, has Cuneiform name *Ḫiši'arša*.

אַרְתַּחְשַׁשְׂתָּא, Ezra, 5, 14, &c. = Artaxerxes; Cuneiform names = *Artakšatsu* and *Artakšasu*.

APPENDIX.

NOTE 1.—The student may consult with great profit a work by Professor Kaulen, of Bonn, entitled, "Assyrien und Babylonien nach den neuesten Entdeckungen:" Freiburg im Breisgau, 2nd edition, 1882. We refer him particularly to chapter vi, which treats of the decipherment of the Cuneiform Inscriptions.

NOTE 2.—On מְרָתַיִם see Delitzsch's "Wo lag das Paradies?" p. 182; and on שׁוֹעַ and קוֹעַ see the same work, pp. 233, *sqq*.

Since writing the above Essay, I learn from my friend Mr. Pinches that certain texts, evidently written at an early epoch, show the proper use of the cases, viz.:—

Nominative = *u*(*m*); Genitive = *i*(*m*); Accusative = *a*(*m*).

1. 

a - na - . . . .

I . . . .

2. 

ṣit . . . .

proceedi . . . .

3. 

lib - b . . . .

offspr . . . .

4. 

ilu A . . . .

the god A . . . .

5. 

ilu . . . .

the godd . . . .

6. 

ilu Ś . . . .

the god . . . .

7. 

ilu N . . . .

the god . . . .

TABLET OF ASSURBANIPAL,

RECORDING THE FLIGHT OF ELAMITE PRINCES TO ASSYRIA.

OBVERSE OR FIRST SIDE. (K, 2867.)

1. 

u - na - ka D.P. Aššur - bani - pal šar . . . .

I Assurbanipal king . . . .

2. 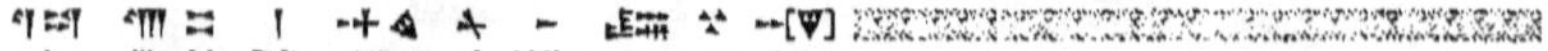

șit lib - bi D.P. Aššur - aḫ - iddina šar mat Aššur . . . .

proceeding from the body of Esarhaddon, king of Assyria . . . .

3. 

lib - bal - bal D.P. Sin - aḫê - irba (?) . . . .

offspring of Sennacherib . . . .

4. 

ilu Aššur ilu Bêlu ilâni iš - di iṣu kussi . . . .

the god Assur, the god Bel, the gods the foundation of the throne . . . .

5. 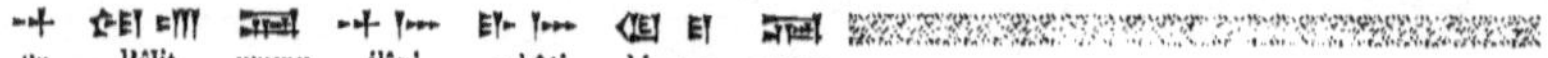

ilu . Bêlit ummu ilâni rabûti ki - ma ummu . . . .

the goddess Beltis, mother of the great gods, like the mother . . . .

6. 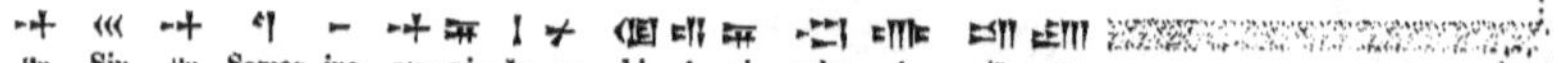

ilu Sin ilu Samas ina au - ni - šu - nu ki - ê - ni arḫu - ú iš - ta . . . .

the god Sin, the god Samas in their grace continual, month . . . .

7. 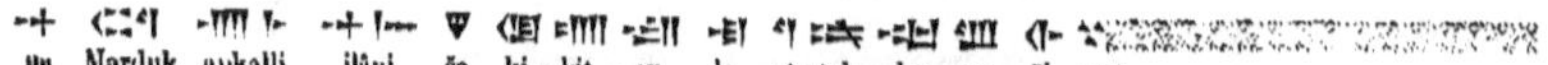

ilu Marduk apkalli ilâni ša ki - bit - su la ut - tak - ka - ru ši - mat . . . .

the god Merodach, prince of the gods, whose commands are not changed, destiny . . . .

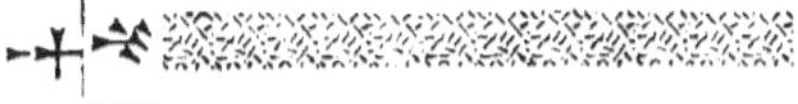

8. 
ilu mu . . . .
the g . . . .

9. 
ilu ṣil - la - ša ṭaba . . . . . .
the *her good protection* . . . . . .

10. 
ilu ša - na - an . . . .
the god *compare* . . . .

11. 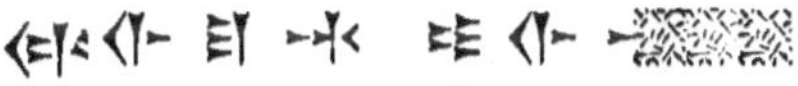
ul ši - ma - ti i - ši -[mu]
the destinies fixed

12. 
ki nu ṣi - ra - a - ti . . .
likereme paths

13. 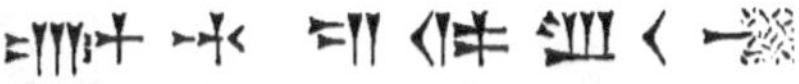
ú an - ti si - di - ru - u . . .
of opposition, ordering . . .

14. 
ú - di ra - bi - ia ig - rum
therity had been hostile to me.

15. 
i - g - ru - u - šu ig - ra - an - ni
th hostile to him was hostile to me.

16. 
ki - ru - du - šu a - di mi -
by [the border of his country]

8. ilu Nabû dup - šar gim - ri aḫ - zi ni - mê - ki - šu ša i - ram mu ....
the god Nebo, the scribe of all, he who possesses his wisdom, which he loves ....

9. ilu Iš - tar a - ši - bat alu Arba - ili ka - bit - ti ilâni rabûti ṣil - la - ša ṭaba ......
the goddess Istar, dwelling in the city of Arbela, the mighty one of the great gods, her good protection ......

10. ilu Nergal dan - dan - ni ilâni dun - nu zik - ru - tu ê - mu - ki la ša - na - an ....
the god Nergal, the strong one of the gods, the strength, manliness, strength without compare ....

11. ul - tu ṣi - ḫi - ri - ia ilâni rabûti a - šib šam - ê u irṣi - tim ši - ma - ti i - ši -[mu]
from my youth up the great gods dwelling in heaven and earth, the destinies fixed

12. ki - ma abi ba - ni - ê ú - rab - bu - in - ni al - ka - kat - ê - šu - nu ṣi - ra - a - ti ...
like the father my begetter they made me great, their supreme paths ...

13. ú - lam - mê - du - in - ni ê - piš ḳabli u taḫâzi di - ku - ut a - na - an - ti si - di - ru - u ...
they taught me the making of fight and battle, the gathering together of opposition, ordering ...

14. ú - šar - bu - u kakki - ia êli amêlu nakri - ia ša ul - tu ṣi - ḫi - ri - ia a - di ra - bi - ia ig - rum
they made great my weapons against mine enemies, who from my youth to my maturity had been hostile to me.

15. i - di - nu di - ê - ni it - ti D.P. Ur - ta - ki šar mat Elamti ša la ag - ru - u - šu ig - ra - an - ni
they delivered judgment against Urtaki, king of Elam, who (though) I was not hostile to him was hostile to me.

16. ki - ê - mu - u - a abikta - šu iš - ku - nu im - ḫa - ṣu pa - na - as - su id - ru - du - šu a - di mi-
by my means(?) his overthrow they caused, they smote his front, they drove him to [the border of his country]

17. 
ina(?) šat Nugia a- šar la
in the Hades, a place not

18. 
lib-bi ka-bat-ti bêlu-ti-šu
the heart honour (?) of his dominion

19. 
šarru- ul- ḳu - u ša-nam (?)
his kingto take, and to another (?)

20. 
Um -ma šar mât Elamti
Umming of Elam,

21. 
Ku-dur-ni Ur- ta - ki
Kudurled Urtaki

22. 
60 zêru ša mât Elamti
sixty of the the land of Elam

23. 
la pa-ba-tu šêpâ šarru[tia]
before the feet of my majesty

24. 
ul-tu ilu E-a ú -paṭ[ṭi-ru]
from [the timeains, the god Ea has set free

17. ina(?) šatti šu-a-tu lim-ni ú-hal-li-ḳu nap-šat-su ip-ḳi-du-šu a-na mât Nugia a-šar la

in that year by an evil omen(?) they destroyed his life, they appointed him to Hades, a place not

18. lib-bi ilâni rabûti bêli-ia ûl i-nu-uḫ ûl ip-šaḫ ša ê-zu-zu ka-bat-ti bêlu-ti-šu

the heart of the great gods my lords was not quiet, was not happy, which strengthened (?) the honour (?) of his dominion

19. šarru-us-su iš-ki-pu pali-šu ê-ki-mu bê-lut mât Elamti ú-šal-ḳu-u ša-nam (?)

his kingdom they overthrew, his dynasty they took away, the dominion of Elam they caused to take, and to another (?)

20. Um-man-i-gas Um-man-ap-pa Tam-ma-ri-tu marâni Ur-ta-ki šar mât Elamti

Ummanigas, Ummanappa, Tammaritu, sons of Urtaki, king of Elam.

21. Ku-dur-ru Pa-ru-u marâni Um-man-al-da-si šarri a-lik pa-ni Ur-ta-ki

Kudurru, Parû, sons of Ummanaldas, the king who preceded Urtaki

22. 60 zêru šarri ina la mê-ni amêlu ṣabâni ḳašti marâni ba-ni-ê ša mât Elamti

sixty of the seed of the king, without number archers, sons, begotten ones of the land of Elam

Reverse or Second Side.

23. la pa-an da-a-ki Te-um-man aḫ abi-šu-nu in-nab-tu-nim-ma iṣ-ba-tu šêpâ šarru[tia]

before the killing of Teumman, the brother of their father, they fled and took the feet of my majesty

24. ul-tu ina iṣu kussi abi ba-ni-ia ú-ši-bu ilu Rammânu zunni-šu ú-maš-ši-ra ilu E-a ú-pat[ti-ru]

from [the time when] on the throne of the father my begetter they set (me), the god Rimmon has let loose his rains, the god Ea has set free

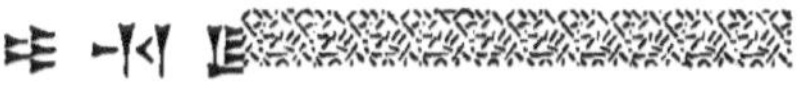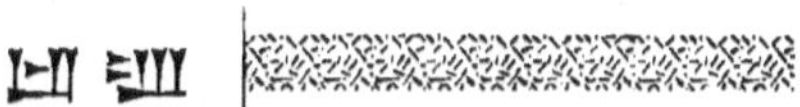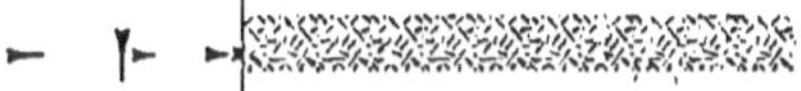

25. 

kištâ -šu-u ni - ri - bu . . .

the grove was no passage . . .

26. 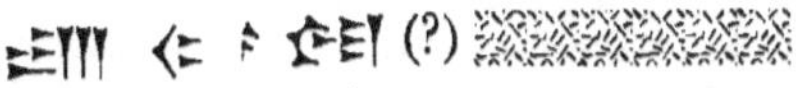

ta - lit - - nin . . . .

the bringer . . . .

27. 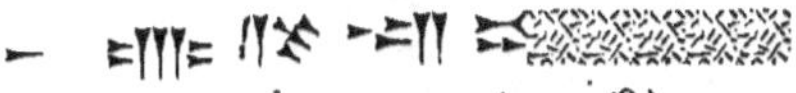

ina ú - zi - zu - tum (?) . . .

as fed . . . .

28. 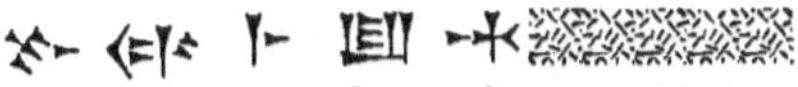

bu - ul mê - lu - ti . . . .

the beast of of men . . . .

29. 

ki - ma u [ṣi - ê - ni]

like the the oxen and sheep

30. 

i - bak - k . . . .

they s . . . .

31. 

i - sa - ap . . . .

they . . . .

32. 

ip - šit . . . .

the . . . .

33. 

ina mê - t . . . .

in the . . . .

25. kištâti -ma iṣu ḳanî ṣu - ṣi - ê uš - tê - li - pu la î -šu-u ni - ri - bu . . .
the groves and the reeds of the plains they caused to sprout forth, there was no passage . . .

26. ta - lit - ti nêši ki - rib ši - in i - šir - ma ina la - a mê - ni ik - uin . . . .
the bringer forth of lions in the midst of them directed, and without number . . . .

27. ina û - kul - ti alpi ṣi - ê ni u a - mê - lu - ti in - na - ad - ru - ma ê - zi - zu - tum (?) . . .
as food, oxen, sheep and men they were destroyed and . . . .

28. bu - ul ṣêri ka - a - a - an û - šam - ḳa - tu i - tab - ba - ku dâmi a - mê - lu - ti . . . .
the beast of the desert constantly caused they to fall, they poured forth the blood of men . . . .

29. ki - ma tap - di - ê ilu Nergal tab - kat ša - lam - tu amêlu bêlî alpi u [ṣi - ê - ni]
like the onset, the god Nergal, the pouring forth of the corpses of dead men, of the oxen and sheep

30. i - bak - ku - û amêlu ri'i amêlu na - ḳi - di ša la ab - bi - ik . . . .
they slew (?) the shepherds, the herdsmen whom I had not slain (?) . . . .

31. i - sa - ap - pi - du da - ad - mê ur - ru u mu - šu . . . .
they . . . . the abodes day and night . . . .

32. ip - šit nêši ša - a - tu - nu iḳ - bu - nim - ma . . . .
the work of those lions they told to me, and . . . .

33. ina mê - ti - iḳ gir - ri - ia ki - rib . . . .
in the course of my expedition, within . . . .

. . . .

. . . .

. . . .

. . . .

. . . .

. . . .

. . . .

. . . .

. .

. .

. . .

.

-𒈨 𒆳 𒉏 𒈠

ah Elamti

ion of Elam.

. . . .

. . . .

. . . .

. . . .

. . . .

. . . .

. . . .

. . . .

ah Elamti

ion of Elam.

34. 
ḳin - na - a - ti - šu - nu ú - par - ri - ir ....
their families I broke to pieces ....

35. 
nišê a - ši - bu - tu alâni [amêlu] ....
the people inhabiting the cities ....

36. 
ina û - mê - šu ša marûni šar ....
at that time of the sons of the king ....

37. 
šá ul - tu ....
who out of ....

On the Left Edge, Right-hand part.

ina rig - mê-šu-nu ḫur - ša - a - ni i - ram ....
with their voices the forests rang ....

iḳ - ṭa - na - lu - du ú - ma - am [ṣêri] ....
they enclosed (?) the wild beast [of the desert].

On the Left Edge, Left-hand part.

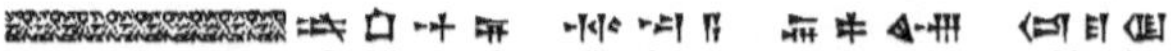
.... - tak - kil - an - ni iḳ - ba - a sa - pa - aḫ Elamti
.... *trusted to me, he ordered the evacuation of Elam.*

NOTES.

1. *anakû* = 1st personal pronoun. *Cf.* the Hebrew form. The final *u* is long: in proof of this see the Sumerian hymn in Haupt's "Akkadische und Keilschrift-texte," line 15 (*a-na-ku-û*), and lines 17 and 19 (*ana-ku-û*).

   Assurbanîpal. 𒁹 is the determinative prefix before the names of persons. 𒀭 = *ilu*, 'god.' *Cf.* אֵל. 𒀭𒊹 is the god Assur (an ideograph), and by these characters as his ideograph the god is represented as *ilu ṭabu* (טוב), 'the kind, good god.' 𒀀 is an ideograph for *aplu* or *mâru*, 'a son;' 𒆕 is an ideograph for *banû*, 'to beget.' Hence from these ideographs we get the name *Assur-bani-pal*, which means 'the god Assur has begotten a son.'

   šar; cstr. state of *šarru*, 'a king.' *Cf.* the Hebrew שַׂר. The character in line 1 is a frequent ideograph for *šarru*. Another ideograph is 𒎙. Sumerian = *šer*.

2. *ṣit*, 𒌓𒁺, is an ideograph for *aṣû*, 'to go out.' *Cf.* Hebrew יָצָא. *See* S[b] 84, where we find that this character = *a-ṣu-u*, i.e., *aṣû*. From this verb we have the noun *ṣitu*, cstr. *ṣit*, which means 'offspring.'

   libbu = heart. *Cf.* לֵב, or better, the form לֵבָב. This phrase is common on the tablets. The Assyrians speak of the offspring of the heart, whereas we speak of the offspring of the body: 'sprung from the body of.' *Cf.* for this phrase the Inscription of Assurbanipal, 5 R, column 2, lines 70, 78, &c. With the use of the verb *aṣu*, or the noun derived from it, in this sense, *cf.* the Hebrew phrase in Gen. xvii, 6, מִמְּךָ יֵצֵאוּ. With יָצָא in Hebrew we find מִיָּרֵךְ and מִבֶּטֶן, as in Assyrian we have *libbu* (לֵב).

Aššur-aḫu-iddina = Esarhaddon. *Cf.* אֵסַרְחַדּוֹן; spoken of in I R 48: Esarhaddon, king of Assyria, son of Sennacherib, king of Assyria. So in our inscription, we have the determinative, then the two characters for the god Assur; the next character, , is an Assyrian abbreviation for *aḫu* (אָח), 'brother,' and  an abbreviation for *iddina*, which is from *nadânu*, 'to give.' The meaning of his name is, 'the god Assur has given a brother.'

mâtu = land. *Cf.* S^b 302; in Akkadian *mâtu* = *kur*. *Cf.* the Chaldee word מָתָא. Its plural = *matâti*.

3. *libbalbal* must mean 'offspring' also. Observe the reduplication in the word. The word *liblibbu*, also having a reduplication, has the same meaning, viz., 'offspring.' (*See* Inscription of Tiglathpileser I, column 7, line 55.) The word *libbalbal* is one that often occurs in the Inscriptions. *See* particularly plate 2 of III R. Tablet I of Sargon, sixth year, reads in line 3, *lib-bal-bal*. And so often on this plate.

Sin-aḫê-irba (?) = Sennacherib (סַנְחֵרִיב). The first two characters stand for the moon-god Sin;  with the sign of the plural number, viz., , we read *'aḫê*, 'brothers.' Assyriologists are not agreed as to how to read the last character, viz., 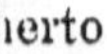. It has been hitherto held that we are to read *irba*, from *rabû*, 'to increase,' for which word this character is an ideograph. Others consider that some such word as *êribu* is to be sought for here. What the word is for which *su* is ideograph has yet to be found; and until the meaning of *su* has been determined, the explanation of the name Sennacherib must be considered as undetermined.

4. The first two characters = the god Assur: the following three represent the name of the god Bêlu, *i.e.*, Bêl. Bel is the exalted one, the father of the gods. *Cf.* the Hebrew name בֵּל in Isaiah xlvi, 1. The plural of *ilu* = *ilâni*. *Cf.* אֵל in Hebrew.

išdu = foundation. Identical with this is the Hebrew אֹשֶׁר. *Išdi* (or *išid*) *kussi* occurs often; *see, e.g.*, the passage referred to by Lotz, viz., II R 38, 32*a*, where we read, *išdi kussi abišu*. In this passage it is represented by its ideograph . *See* the remarks on Hebrew Lexicography in regard to the word *kussu* = כִּסֵּא.

5. *Bêlit*; wife of Bel, and mother of the gods.

ummu = the Hebrew אֵם, 'mother.' The word is undoubtedly from a root אמם. It is here represented by its ideograph. The Akkadian for *ummu* is *a-ma*. Cstr. = *um*.

rabû, plural *rabûti* = great. With this may be compared the Hebrew רַב in the compound word רַבְשָׁקֵה. רַב, in *pausa* רָב = many, much, great. In the text it is represented by its ideograph. *See* II R 1, No. 123.

kima = 'like,' as corresponding to the Hebrew כְּ.

6. *Sin* is the moon-god, the national god of the old town of Ur. The character 𒌍 is also the representative of the numeral 30. Hence the god Sin, according to this ideograph, is the god of 30 (days), or a month: the month-god.

Samas is the Hebrew שֶׁמֶשׁ, 'sun,' the sun-god; 𒌓 is also an ideograph for *ûmu* (יוֹם), 'day.' Thus Samas is the god of *day, i.e.*, the sun. Worshipped in Sippar.

anni-šunu = their grace; *annu* = Hebrew חֵן, *i.e.*, the root of the Assyrian word is חנן; the *a* is ה_3; *šunu* is 3rd plural masc. suffix.

ki-ê-ni, i.e., *kêni*, is an adjective agreeing in case with *anni*; its root is כון, and connected with this it must mean 'faithful, constant.' Nebo is the *kênu ablu* of Merodach.

7. *apkallu*, or *apgallu*, is most likely from the Akkadian, meaning, 'great father.' *See* an interesting note on this word by Mr. Pinches in the "Trans. Soc. Bib. Arch.," Vol. VII, Part 2, 1881, in his article entitled "A new Fragment of the History of Nebuchadnezzar III."

Marduk = the god Merodach, in Hebrew מְרֹדַךְ. *See* this name of the god in the compound name Merodach-Baladan. This god is the herald of the gods, the *apkallu*, and the first-born son of the god Ea.

ša- . . . . . . *su* = literally 'which . . . . . . his,' *i.e.*, whose. Of the Hebrew custom of joining the relative pronoun to the suffix of the following noun, *see* Gesenius's Grammar, § 123.

kibit, for *ḳibit*, and this from *ḳibtu*, 'order, or command;' *ḳibit* is the form of the word used before suffixes. *Ḳibtu*, from a verb *ḳabû*. *Cf.* the Aramaic verb קְבַע.

uttakkaru, from the verb *nakâru*, 'to change,' II, 2 (*i.e.*, Iftaal), present; *nakâru* means 'to tear down, to change:' whence *nakru*, 'an enemy.' The root נכר means 'to be strange, hostile.' *Cf.* the Hebrew; also the Æthiopic *nakara* in II, ₁ = *peregrinum invenit*, and adjective *nakîr* = *alienus*.

la is the adverb of negation. *Cf.* Hebrew לֹא; also the Syriac *lâ*, and Chaldee לָא.

šîmat is construct state of *šîmtu*, 'fate or destiny.' The root is שִׂים, 'to fix, to appoint.' *Šîmtum* = the Arab. شِيمَةٌ.

8. *Nabû* is god Nebo, the originator of the art of writing, and hence called in our text *dupšar gimri*. *Cf.* נְבוֹ.

dupšar, cstr. of *dupšarru*. *See* Hebrew Lexicography on this word.

gimru, totality (*Gesammtheit*); from a root גמר, 'to be complete.' *Cf.* the Æthiopic *gamara* and the Syriac *gĕmâr*, '*perfectum et integrum esse*.' Construct state of *gimru* is *gimir*.

aḫzi; root is אָחַז, 'to seize, possess.' Here in the construct state before *nîmêki*, 'wisdom.' *Bêl nîmêki*, *i.e.*, 'the lord of wisdom unfathomable,' is a title of the god Ea. In the great Nebuchadnezzar Inscription published in I R, plates 59–64, we read in column I, line 7, *a-ḫi-iz ni-mé-ki*, 'the possessor of wisdom.'

râmu, 'to love;' root is רא$_3$ם, *i.e.*, the Arabic رَحِمَ; here Ḳal, 3rd person singular. The plural is *iramu*.

9. *Ištar*, *i.e.*, Astarte. In the Inscriptions we read of *Ištar ša Ninua*, and *Ištar ša Arba'-ili*, *i.e.*, 'Istar of Niniveh, and Istar of Arbela;' and on an inscription of Esarhaddon (marked No. 15, and found 19th July, 1880), line 5, in column 1, we read, 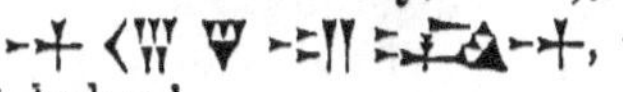, *i.e.*, *Ištar ša Bâbîli*, 'Istar of Babylon.'

ašibat, cstr. state of the word *ašibûtu*, fem. part. of the masc. *ašibu*, which is Ḳal of the verb *ašâbu*, 'to dwell.' *Cf.* with this verb the Hebrew יָשַׁב.

Arba-'ilu = Arbela; the two characters mean *four*, *god*. We know from our text and from other inscriptions that *Ištar* was worshipped there.

Kabittu; fem. of *kabtu;* 'heavy, honourable, mighty.' *Cf.* כָּבֵד.

ṣilla; accusat. of *ṣillu*, 'shadow, protection;' *Cf.* צֵל; *ša* is here the third feminine singular suffix. *Ṭabu* = good. *Cf.* טוֹב.

10. *dandannu*, a reduplicated form from *dannu*, 'mighty.' In this text we have had one other such form, viz., *libbalbal*.

Zikrûtu; abstract noun from *zikaru*, 'manly, male,' as opposed to female. The Hebrew adjective is זָכָר; female = *zinništu*.

dunnu, 'strength;' undoubtedly connected with *danânu*, 'to be strong, powerful.'

emûḳu, 'might, forces.' Root א$_4$מק. Schrader correctly compares with this word the Hebrew עָמַק, 'to be deep;' *emûḳu* is originally 'the deep.'

la šanan; a common phrase in the Inscriptions. *See* Delitzsch, in Lotz's "Tiglathpileser," on the phrase, page 102.

Nergal is described in this line as the strong one of the gods, whose manly strength is without compare. *See* Delitzsch, in his edition of Smith's "Chaldean Genesis," pp. 274–276, on the name of this god.

11. *ultu*='out of;' a preposition common in Assyrian.

ṣiḫiru = 'youth;' from the adjective *ṣiḫru*, 'small, young.' To it is added the 1st singular suffix *ia* or *a*. Root is צחר.

šâmê, 'heaven.' *Cf.* שָׁמַיִם. The *ê* is here phonetic complement; 𒀭 is ideograph for *ilu* as well as *šâmu*.

irṣitu, 'earth.' *Cf.* אֶרֶץ; *tim* or *ti* is phonetic complement.

išîmu; Ḳal, 3rd plur. masc. *šâmu*, 'to fix.' *Cf.* Hebrew שִׂים.

12. *abu*, 'father' = אָב; 𒀜 is ideograph for *abu;* here in genitive.

ba-ni-ê, i.e., *banê;* genitive case (*cf. šâmê*, which is also genitive, like *irṣiti*), from *banû* = 'begetter.' The verb *banû* = 'to build, create, beget.' With the verb *cf.* בָּנָה.

urabbu-inni; from *rabû*, 'to be great,' the Piel form, which is causative of Ḳal, and means 'to make great;' here in 3rd plur. masc. with *inni*, the 1st singular suffix.

ṣîrâti; plural fem. of *ṣîru*, 'exalted, supreme.' The form is فُعُل. (*See* Haupt's "Sumerische Familien-Gesetze," page 5, note 3.)

alkakâti. I translate this word *paths*. It occurs in IV R, plate 15, line 60, where we have *al-ka-ka-a-ti si-bit-ti-šu-nu.*

13. *ulammêdu-inni;* למד, 'to learn;' here the 3rd plur. masc. with 1st personal suffix.

êpiš; verb *primæ gutturalis*, from *êpîšu*, 'to make.' Participle = *epišu;* Present = *êppuš;* Imperfect = *êpuš.*

ḳabli and *taḫazi* are here ideographs. *See* for *ḳabli*, S^b 88, or II R. 1, 87; and for *taḫazi*, *see* II R, 2, 291, where we have *ta-ḫa-[zu]*. Construct of *ḳablu* is *ḳa-bal.*

dikûtu: abstract noun; from *dakû*, 'to gather;' *dikut* is in construct state. The root is דכי.

anantu; a synonym of *tukuntu*, II R, 29, 53; and IV R, 26, 13, where we have *dikû* (not *dišû*) *anantum.* (Communicated to me by Mr. Pinches.)

sidirû; 'to order, arrange.' *Cf.* Chaldee סְדַר = Hebrew עָרַךְ, 'to set in a row.' *Sidru* = 'arrangement.'

14. *ušarbû;* from *rabû*, 'to be great;' here it is the Schaphel, or causative form, imperfect 3rd plur. masc., 'to cause to be great, make great.'

kakkîa; the plural of *kakku*, with the 1st person pronominal suffix *ia* or *a*. *Kakku* means 'a weapon;' *iṣu* is a determinative prefix; is the usual ideograph for this word.

êli; preposition, 'against.' *Cf.* with it the prepositions in Hebrew and Arabic, viz., עַל and عَلَى.

nakru, with the determinative prefix *amêlu*, 'man' = 'enemy;' *nakrîa* = 'mine enemies.' *Cf.* in line 7 the verb *nakâru*, 'to be hostile.'

ša; the Assyrian relative pronoun; *adi* = Latin *cum.*

rabû; this is here the exact contrary of *ṣiḫirîa*, and must mean *maturity.* צחר = 'small, young;' and so *rabû* = 'great, mature.'

15. *dênu*, or *dînu*, 'judgment, council;' in our text syllabically written. Its ideograph is . *Cf.* the Contract Tablets in III R, plate 46, lines 18, &c., where *dênu* is a word of frequent occurrence. *Cf.* further with this word the Hebrew דִּין, judgment. So also in the Chaldee, in Syriac; in Æthiopic *dain* = *damnatio, judicium*, &c.

idinu; verb *mediæ Vav*, imperfect Ḳal, 3rd plur. masc., from *dânu*, 'to judge;' here used with a cognate accusative.

itti; a preposition, 'with' = אֵת in Hebrew.

Urtaki; also mentioned in the Annals of Assurbanipal, V R, column 3, line 44, where we read of "Ummanigas, son of Urtaki, king of Elam."

agru; a verb from *gâru,* 'to be hostile;' related to the Hebrew root גָּר ; *šu* is 3rd person verbal suffix, and *anni* is 1st pronominal suffix.

16. *kêmâa* must mean something like 'by my means;' *a* is probably the 1st person pronominal suffix.

abiktu, 'overthrow;' the above two characters are its usual ideograph. Along with *iškun,* thus, *iškun abikta-šu,* it is a common phrase in the historical inscriptions. *See* Lotz's "Tiglathpileser," page 114.

iškunû; from *šakânu,* 'to cause, make;' imperfect Ḳal, 3rd plur. masc. Schrader compares כון and Haupt שָׁכַן.

imḫaṣû; imperfect I, 3rd plur., from *maḫâṣu,* 'to fight, smite.' *Cf.* מָחַץ. Its Ifteal, *amdaḫḫiṣ,* occurs often.

panassu = *panat-su.* *Cf.* IV R 53, 15, where we read, *i-na pa-na-at niši;* *panâtu* is 'the front, the face;' *su* or *šu* is 3rd pronominal suffix singular.

idrudû-šu; 3rd plur. masc., imperfect Ḳal, from a root *darâdu;* may be connected with the root טרד, whose root-meaning is 'drive, force.' If this be so, then *idrudû* = *iṭrudû.* Smith translates it, "they drove him to [the border of his country]."

17. *šattu;* the above three characters, *mu, an, na,* are its ideograph; *šattu* = *šantu,* 'year.' *Cf.* the Hebrew שָׁנָה.

šuatu; demonstrative pronoun sing. = 'that.' Plural is *šuatûnu.* ►►◄ = *nabû* (II R 7, 37*g, h*), or we may take ►— as the preposition *ina,* ►◄ (with which every omen in the portent-tablets begins), as meaning *omen.* The characters however are much too closely written in the original to allow of their being separated.

limnu; adjective = 'evil, wicked;' its feminine is *limuttu* = *limuntu.* Status cstr. = *limun.*

uḫalliḳu; Piel, imperfect 3rd plur., from *ḫalâḳu,* 'to destroy.'

napšatsu. *Cf.* נֶפֶשׁ, 'soul;' *napištu,* cstr. *napšat,* is Assyrian word. *Su* is 3rd masc. suffix.

ipḳidû. With this word I compare פָּקַד, 'to decree, hand over, punish.' *Cf.* further the Syriac ܦܩܰܕ *jussit, imperavit*.

Nugia, *i.e.*, Hades, is explained as *irṣit la tarat*, 'the land whence is no return.' *Cf.* with this the well-known "Descent of Istar to Hades," line 1, where we read, *a-na mât Nu-gi-a*, *i.e.*, "to the land, &c." *Nu* is the Akkadian negative particle; 𒃻𒄩 has the ideographic value *târu*, 'to return,' so that *Nugia* means 'non-return.'

ašar; estr. state of *ašru*, 'place.' *Cf.* Aramaic אֲתַר, the Syriac ܐܰܬܪܳܐ, the Arabic أَثَرٌ, and the Æthiopic አሰር, '*vestigium*.'

18. *inuḫ*; from *nâḫu*, 'to rest, be quiet.' Verb *Mediæ Vav*, Ḳal imperfect 3rd sing. masc. *Cf.* נוּחַ in Hebrew.

ipšaḫ; from *pašâḫu*, 'to be happy, be quiet.' *Cf.* Æthiopic ፈሥሐ, and Syriac ܦܨܰܚ, '*hilaris, beatus fuit*.'

ezuzu, 'to strengthen;' connected, I imagine, with *izzu*, 'strong.' The root is עזז.

kabattu may mean 'honour,' or perhaps like ክብድ (*kebad*), *amplitudo*.

bêlutu, 'dominion, kingdom;' formed from *bêlu*, 'lord.'

19. *šarrussu* = *šarrut-su* = *šarrûti-su* = *šarrûti-šu* = 'his kingdom;' formed from *šarru*, 'king.'

iškipu, for *iškipu*; from *šaḳâpu*, 'to overthrow.'

pališu, 'his reign or dynasty;' 𒁀𒌋 is the usual ideogram for *palu*, 'reign.' Probably of Akkadian origin.

êkimu, 'to take away.' *Cf.* IV R, column 3, line 116, where we read, *a-na ê-kîm ma-ḫa-zi šu-bat ilâni rabûti*, "in order to take away the towns, the seats of the great gods." Here it is Ḳal 3rd plur. masc.

ušalḳû; Schaphel, from the root לָקַח, 'to take,' imperfect 3rd plur. masc.

ša-[nam-ma]. If the last character in the line be *nam*, the word may be *ša-nam-[ma]*, *i.e.*, 'to another.' Nominative, *šanumma*; genitive, *šanimma*; accusative, *šanamma*; is the usual indefinite pronoun for 'another,' *irgend ein andrer*.

20. *Ummanigas*. *Cf.* V R 3, 44, in the Inscription of Assurbanipal. *Ummanappa* is not mentioned in V R. Tammaritu (V R 3, 48), called *aha-šu šal-ša-a-a*, *i.e.*, 'the brother, third in rank.' (So Delitzsch.) Our text seems to favour the translation made by Smith, 'the third brother.' Tammaritu ascended the throne of Elam after Ummanigas (V R 4, 3–4).

21. In V R 4, 110–113, we are told that "in his seventh expedition, Assurbanipal directed his march against Ummanaldas, king of the land Elam."

alik, from *alâku*, 'to go.' *Cf.* Hebrew הָלַךְ. Participle = *aliku*. Together with *pani* (*cf.* פָּנִים), it means 'to go before, precede.'

22. *zêru* = זרע, 'seed, offspring.' Its ideograph is . *See* Sayce's Grammar on the mode of reckoning current among the Assyrians.

ina la mêni; literally 'in not number,' *i.e.*, without number. *Cf.* the Hebrew phrase, עַד אֵין מִסְפָּר, Job ix, 10; *ina la* = the Hebrew בְּלֹא. *See* further, Ewald's Syntax, § 286*g*.

ṣâbâni; plural of *ṣabu*, whose ideograph is , = 'men, warriors.' *Cf.* with this word the Æthiopic *ṣabâ'i*, '*bellator, bellicosus*.' The plural is *ṣâbâni*, not *ṣâbî*. (Lotz, "Tiglathpileser I," 101.)

ḳašti. *Cf.* קֶשֶׁת, 'bow;' *šabâni ḳašti* = 'men of the bow,' *i.e.*, *archers*. *Ḳaštu*, estr. *ḳašat*, plur. *ḳašâti* = 'bow.'

banî-ê; the *ê* is phonetic complement, showing us that we are to read *banê*, not *banî*; from the root *banû*, 'to beget, build.'

Reverse Side.

23. *la-pa-an;* preposition = before. *Cf.* לִפְנֵי.

dâku, 'to kill.' A verb *mediæ Vav* of the root דּוּךְ. Here it is a *nomen actionis.*

Teumman; also mentioned in Annals of Assurbanipal, V R, column 3. His brother Urtaki, who preceded him on the throne of Elam, committed suicide. Teumman had always been a bitter enemy of Assyria, and "the leader in every action against her interests." On this portion of Assyrian history I would refer the reader to the short history of Assyria by the late George Smith, pp. 155–160.

abišunu; from *abu,* 'father;' with 3rd plural pronominal suffix. *Cf.* the Hebrew אָב.

innabtunimma = innabtuni + ma; from *abâtu,* 'to flee;' Niphal 3rd plural (full form) masc. (*See* Haupt, "Sumerische Familien-Gesetze," page 10); *ma* is the conjunction *and.*

iṣbatû; from *ṣabâtu,* 'to seize, lay hold of;' imperfect Ḳal, 3rd plur. masc. Last edition of Gesenius gives צבת in Chaldee, perhaps 'seize with the hand.' This is undoubtedly the meaning of the root in Assyrian.

šêpû, 'foot.' The 𒈫 on the right-hand side of the character is a dual sign. The laying hold of the feet was a token of submission.

24. *ušibû;* a verb *primæ Vav* (וישב), imperfect Ḳal, 3rd plural, from *ašâbu,* 'to sit, dwell.' Here it means "they (the gods) set me." This can only be the 3rd plural; 3rd singular and 1st singular = *ušib.*

Rammânu (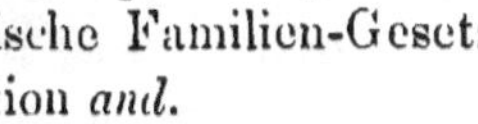) is the god Rimmon. The root is רמם, 'to strike.' *Cf.* the hymn to Rimmon in IV R 28, 18, where we read, *ana šâgimišu, ana ramimišu.* He is the Thunder-god. As the root is רמם, I prefer the view that Rimmon is the hurler of the thunderbolt.

If we take the root to be רום, Rimmon is the 'high and exalted god.' (*See* Delitzsch, in "Chaldäische Genesis," page 269.)

zunnu, 'rain;' literally 'water of heaven.'  is ideograph for water, and  for *šâmu*, 'heaven;' so that 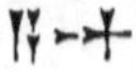 = *rain*, *i.e.*, water + heaven, water from heaven.

umaššira; Piel, imperfect, from *mašâru*, 'to let loose.'

upaṭ[tiru]; thus I complete the word; also Piel, imperfect, from *paṭâru*, 'to set free.' Root is פטר (فطر), 'to split, cause to burst forth.'

25. *kištâti;* plural of *kištu*, 'grove;' in the text is the ideograph with plural sign.

ḳanî (*see* on Hebrew Lexicography); plural of *ḳanû*, 'a reed.'  is its ideograph.

ṣuṣê, 'plains;' plural of *ṣuṣu*. *Cf.* Haupt's "A. S. K.," p. 33, No. 771, with II R, 8, 30*c*, *d*.

uštêlipu; Schaphel, imperfect 3rd plur. masc., from the root חלף, 'to pierce;' in text = 'cause to sprout forth. *Cf.* II R 36, 66–68, where we have *e-li-pu; e-li-pu ša iṣu; ul-lu-pu; elipu ša iṣu* = 'to sprout forth, of wood.'

niribu, 'passage;' a noun, with preformative *Nun*, from *erêbu*, 'to enter.' The root of the verb is ערב.

26. *talitti* = *talidti;* from *alâdu*, 'to bear, bring forth' = 'the bringer forth; German, *Gebärerin*.' A noun, with preformative *Tau*, from a verb *primæ Yod*.

nêšî, 'lions.'  is the ideograph for *kalbu* (כֶּלֶב), 'a dog;'  is an ideograph for *rabû*, 'great.' The two characters together form ideograph for *nêšû*, 'lion;' *i.e.*, 'lion' = great + dog, *i.e.*, 'the great dog.' *Cf.* with this word the Arabic نَبُوس; 'lioness' = *nêštum*. *Cf.* نَهْشَة.

kirib-šin; kirib is a preposition, 'in the midst of, within' (קֶרֶב), and *šin* is 3rd plur. fem. suffix.

išir, for *ašâru*, 'to direct.' Verb *primæ Vav* imperfect Ḳal. *Cf.* Hebrew יָשַׁר.

27. *ukultu*, 'food;' from *akâlu*, 'to eat.' (*Cf.* אָכַל.) *Cf.* II R 60, reverse, line 48, *minû ûkultaka*, 'what is thy food?'

Alpî, plural of *alpû*. 'an ox.' *Cf.* אֶלֶף.

ṣi-ê-ni, i.e., *ṣênî*, 'sheep, small cattle.' *Cf.* צֹאן (*Kleinvieh*).

amelûti; plural of *amêlu*, 'man,' a word borrowed from Sumerian *mulu;* in Kassiti man = *meli;* in Akkadian *lu* (evidently a shortened form).

innadrû-ma; *ma* is the enclytic; innadru is Niphal form of *adâru* (*cf.* the form *innabtû*, from *abâtu*), used of the affliction of the moon-god. (Haupt, "Keilschrifttexte," pp. 76 and 77, line 2, *na-an-dur-šu*, which Professor Delitzsch translated *Bedrängniss*, and derived from a verb *adaru*, 'to fear, afflict.') Our word is 3rd plur. masc. We may translate, 'they were afflicted, or oppressed.'

ezizutu, 'resting place;' perhaps connected with *nazâzu*.

28. *bûl* = 'beast.' *Cf.* בְּהֵמָה. *Cf.* Delitzsch's "Lesestücke," page 79, line 4, where we read, *bu-ul ṣêri u-ma-am ṣêri.*

ṣêri, 'desert;' *scriptio plena* = *ṣi-ê-ru*, i.e., *ṣêru*. *Cf.* the Arabic صَحْرَاء; not to be confounded with *ṣiru*, 'exalted.' II R 8, 27, *c d*, gives  = *ṣi-ê-rum.*

kân; generally translated 'always, constantly.' *Cf.* V R, column 2, line 3.

ušamkatû; Schaphel, imperfect 3rd plur. masc., from *makâtu*, 'to fall.' *Cf.* the Arabic سقط.

itabbakû; from *tabâku*, 'to pour forth.' *Cf.* S[c], 35–37, where we have three synonyms, viz.; *šapaku*, *tabaku*, *sarâku;* here it is Piel, imperfect 3rd plur. masc.

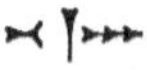 = *dâmî*, 'blood' דָּם *See* S[b], 223.

29. *tapdê;* noun from *padû*, a synonym of *âṣû*, 'to come, or rush forth.' *Cf.* פדה, 'to loose.' *Tap-du-ú* occurs in K 2329, reverse, as given by Mr. Pinches in his "Texts in the Babylonian Wedge-Writing," plate 20, line 4.

šalamtu; synonym of *pagru* (פֶּגֶר); 'a corpse.' *Cf.* V R 3, 8, where we have *ša-lam-ta-šu.*

30. *ibakkû;* from *bakû* (*cf.* בָּכָה), to weep.' Here Piel, 'cause to weep,' and then perhaps 'to slay.' *Abbik* is Niphal, 1st person singular. It occurs in a bilingual list after *dâku,* 'to kill,' and *rapâdu,* 'to lie down.'

ri'î; plural of *ri'u,* 'shepherd.' *Cf.* רֹעֶה. 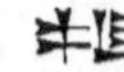 is its ideograph. *See* II R 2, 345; S[b], 203. Original form is *rê'û.* *Cf.* S[c] 308.

naḳidu is the נֹקֵד of Amos i, 1, *i.e.,* 'herdsman.' *Cf.* also Delitzsch's "Lesestücke," page 81, line 25, where we have these same two words together, viz., *ri'î u na-ḳi-di,* and as a variant of *ḳi-di* is given  *kid* or *ḳid.*

31. *dadmê,* 'abodes;' from *dadmû.*

urru, 'light.' *Cf.* אוֹר. *Mûšu,* the usual word for 'night.' *Cf.* Delitzsch's "Lesestücke," page 79, line 13, where we read, *šuknât mûši,* 'the spheres of night.'

32. *ipšit;* construct state of *epištu,* 'work;' from the verb *epîšu,* 'to do.'

iḳbunimma = *iḳbuni* + *ma;* *iḳbuni* = 3rd plur. masc. imperfect Kal, from *ḳabû,* 'to tell,' a verb *tertiæ infirmæ; ni* is here the 1st person sing. suffix. In the text K 3283, line 3, which I copied in the British Museum, we read, 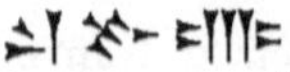 *ḳabû* and not *ḳibû.* In lines 3 and 4 of this text occurs the words:—

Ḳa-bu-ú u la še-mu-ú, &c.
Ša-su-ú u la a-pa-lu(m).

mêtiḳ; construct state of *mêteḳu,* 'march, course, expedition,' from *etêḳu,* 'to advance.' *Cf.* עָתַק.

girrîa; from *girru,* 'campaign, expedition.' + *ia,* 1st person suffix. *Girru* is synonym of *ḫarranu,* 'a way.'

31–37. *ḳinnâti,* 'families;' plural of *ḳinnu,* 'nest, family.' Hebrew קֵן. The root is קנן.

uparrir; from *parâru*, 'to break to pieces.' Imperfect Piel, 1st person singular. *Cf.* Hebrew פָּרַר.

niši; plural of *nišu*, 'the people.' See S^b 246, where 𒌋𒐊 is ideograph for *ni-šu*. With the plural *niši* agrees the participle *ašibûtu*, from *ašâbu*, 'to dwell.'

ûmê; plural of *ûmu*, 'day.' 𒌓 is ideograph for *ûmu* (S^b 81), and *mé* is phonetic complement showing that we are to read here *ûmé*. S^b 81 gives 𒌓-*mu*; and 𒌓 has the syllabic value *u*, according to S^a 2, 10. (*See* Haupt, "Sumerische Familien-Gesetze," p. 21.)

ultu = 'out of, *ex*.' What follows *ultu* on the tablet is not clear.

Further Notes.

rigmê-šunu; I read *rigmê*, the plural of *rigmu*, 'word, voice,' from *ragâmu*, 'to speak' [*Cf.* S^c 317, 320, or IV R 70, 58–61], a synonym of *ḳabû* (קָבַע), 'to command.'

ḫuršâni; plural of *ḫuršu*, 'forest' = Hebrew חֹרֶשׁ.

iḳtanaladu; root is قلد, 'to enclose, collect,' from a verb *ḳaladu*, the Iftaneal form imperfect 3rd plural, and for *iḳtanaladu*.

úmâm. *Cf.* line 28; corresponds to חַיָּה in Hebrew, and means 'wild beast.' *Umâm* is status cstr. of *umâmu*.

[*u*]*takkilanni*; from the verb *takâlu*, 'to trust,' Piel, Imperfect 3rd sing. masc. with 1st singular verbal suffix *anni*.

sapaḫ; from *sapâḫu*, 'to evacuate.' With this word I compare the Syriac ܣܦܚ and the Arabic سَفَحَ, *effudit*; and then *evacuavit*. Here *sapaḫ* is in status cstr.

HARRISON AND SONS,
PRINTERS IN ORDINARY TO HER MAJESTY,
ST. MARTIN'S LANE, LONDON.

14, Henrietta Street, Covent Garden, London;
20, South Frederick Street, Edinburgh.

CATALOGUE

OF

WILLIAMS AND NORGATE'S PUBLICATIONS.

Abhidhanaratnamala, the, of Halâyudha. A Sanskrit Vocabulary (120 pp.), edited, with a complete Sanskrit-English Glossary (180 pp.), by Dr. T. Aufrecht. 8vo. (Published at 18*s*.) 10*s*.

Æschylus. Agamemnon. Greek Text revised and translated by John F. Davies, B.A. 8vo, cloth. 3*s*.

Ali (Syed Ameer) Life of Mohammed. A Critical Examination of the Life and Teachings of Mohammed, from a Mohammedan Standpoint, including Chapters on Polygamy, Slavery, Moslem Rationalism, Moslem Mysticism, &c. Crown 8vo, cloth. 9*s*.

Attwell (Professor H.) Table of Aryan (Indo-European) Languages, showing their Classification and Affinities, with copious Notes; to which is added, Grimm's Law of the Interchange of Mute Consonants, with numerous Illustrations. A Wall Map for the use of Colleges and Lecture-rooms. 2nd Edition. Mounted with rollers. 10*s*.

—— **Table of the Aryan Languages,** with Notes and Illustrations. 4to, boards. 7*s*. 6*d*.

Autobiography of an Independent Minister, Chapters from the. Cr. 8vo, cloth, 4*s*.

Bannister (Rev. Dr. J.) Glossary of Cornish Names, Ancient and Modern, Local, Family, Personal, 20,000 Celtic and other Names in use in Cornwall. 8vo, cloth. 12*s*.

Barnabas' Epistle, in Greek, from the Sinaitic Manuscript of the Bible, with a Translation by S. Sharpe. Crown 8vo, cloth. 2*s*. 6*d*.

Barratt (A.) Physical Ethics, or the Science of Action: an Essay. 8vo, cloth. 12*s*.

Baur (F. C.) Church History of the First Three Centuries. Translated from the Third German Edition. Edited by Rev. Allan Menzies. 2 vols. 8vo, cloth. 21*s*.

—— **Paul, the Apostle of Jesus Christ,** his Life and Work, his Epistles and Doctrine. A Contribution to a Critical History of Primitive Christianity. Translated by Rev. A. Menzies. 2 vols. 8vo, cloth. 21*s*.

Bayldon (Rev. G.) Icelandic Grammar. An Elementary Grammar of the Old Norse or Icelandic Language. 8vo, cl. 7*s*. 6*d*.

Beard (Rev. C.) Port Royal, a Contribution to the History of Religion and Literature in France. 2 vols. 8vo. 12*s*.

Bernstein and Kirsch. Syriac Chrestomathy and Lexicon. Chrestomathia Syriaca cum Lexico. 2 vols. in 1. 8vo, cloth. 7*s*. 6*d*.

Bible, translated by Samuel Sharpe, being a Revision of the Authorized English Version. 5th Edition of the Old Testament, 9th Edition of the New Testament. 8vo, roan. 4*s*. 6*d*.

—— vide also Testament.

Bible for Young People. A Critical, Historical, and Moral Handbook to the Old and New Testaments. By Dr. H. Oort and Dr. J. Hooykaas, with the assistance of Dr. Kuenen. Translated from the Dutch by the Rev. P. H. Wicksteed. 6 vols. Crown 8vo. 31*s*.

Bisset (A.) Short History of the English Parliament. Crown 8vo. 4*s*.

Bleek (F.) Lectures on the Apocalypse. Edited by Dr. S. Davidson. 8vo, cloth. 10*s*. 6*d*.

Bouzique (E. U.) The History of Christianity. Translated from the French by the Rev. Dr. Beard. 3 vols. Crown 8vo, cloth. 21*s*.

Bryce (Rev. Dr.) The Laws of Greek Accentuation simplified. 3rd Edition. 12mo. 6*d*.

Channing and Lucy Aikin. Correspondence of William Ellery Channing, D.D., and Lucy Aikin, from 1826 to 1842. Edited by Anna Letitia Le Breton. Crown 8vo, cloth. (Published at 9*s*.) 4*s*.

Chastel (Rev. E.) Christianity in the Nineteenth Century. Translated by the Rev. Dr. Beard. Crown 8vo, cloth. 5*s*.

Cholmondeley (Canon Charles) The Passage of the Four ΓΑΡ. A New Explanation of Romans ii. 11—16, with its bearing on the Intrinsic and Extrinsic Systems of Justification by Faith, and on the Pauline Views of the Tübingen Critics and others. 8vo, cloth. 7*s*. 6*d*.

Cobbe (Miss F. Power) The Peak in Darien, and other Inquiries touching Concerns of the Soul and the Body. Crown 8vo, cloth. 7*s*. 6*d*.

—— **The Duties of Women.** A Course of Lectures delivered in London and Clifton. 2nd Edition. Crown 8vo, cloth. 5*s*.

—— **The Hopes of the Human Race,** Hereafter and Here. Essays on the Life after Death. With a Preface having special reference to Mr. Mill's Essay on Religion. 2nd Edition. Cr. 8vo. 5*s*.

Cobbe (Miss F. Power) Alone to the Alone. Prayers for Theists, by several Contributors. 3rd Edition. Crown 8vo, cloth. 5*s*.

—— **Broken Lights.** An Inquiry into the Present Condition and Future Prospects of Religious Faith. 3rd Edition. 5*s*.

—— **Dawning Lights.** An Inquiry concerning the Secular Results of the New Reformation. 8vo, cloth. 5*s*.

—— **Darwinism in Morals,** and (13) other Essays (Religion in Childhood, Unconscious Cerebration, Dreams, the Devil, Auricular Confession, &c. &c.). 8vo, cloth. 5*s*.

Crawford (Rev. F.) Horæ Hebraicæ. Cr. 8vo, cloth. 4*s*. 6*d*.

Crowfoot (J. R.) Fragmenta Evangelica quæ ex antiqua recens. vers. Syriac. Nov. Test. a Curetono vulg. Græce reddita, &c. 2 Parts; and Observations, 1 Part. 4to. 20*s*.

Cureton (Dr. W.) History of the Martyrs in Palestine, by Eusebius, in Syriac. Edited and translated. Royal 8vo, cloth. 10*s*. 6*d*.

Dante's Inferno. Translated into Greek verse by Mussurus Pasha, D.C.L. 8vo, cloth. 12*s*.

Davids (T. W. Rhys) Lectures on the Origin and Growth of Religion, as illustrated by some Points in the History of Indian Buddhism. (Hibbert Lectures, 1881.) 8vo, cloth. 10*s*. 6*d*.

Davidson (Rev. Dr.) On a Fresh Revision of the English Old Testament. Crown 8vo. 5*s*.

Delbos (Prof. Léon) Chapters on the Science of Language. Crown 8vo, cloth. 3*s*.

Dipavamsa, the: a Buddhist Historical Record in the Pali Language. Edited, with an English Translation, by Dr. H. Oldenberg. 8vo, cloth. 21*s*.

Dunkin (E., F.R.S.) Obituary Notices of Astronomers, Fellows and Associates of the Royal Astronomical Society. 8vo, cloth. 6*s*. 6*d*.

Echoes of Holy Thoughts: arranged as Private Meditations before a First Communion. 2nd Edition, with a Preface by Rev. J. Hamilton Thom. Printed with red lines. Fcap. 8vo, cloth. 2*s*. 6*d*.

Engelhardt (C.) Denmark in the Early Iron Age. Illustrated by recent Discoveries in the Peat-Mosses of Slesvig. 33 Plates (giving representations of upwards of a thousand objects), Maps, and numerous other Illustrations on wood. 4to, cloth. 31*s*. 6*d*.

Ereuna, or an Investigation of the Etymons of Words and Names, Classical and Scriptural, through the Medium of Celtic; together with some Remarks on Hebræo-Celtic Affinities. By a Celtophile. Crown 8vo, cloth. 6*s*.

Ewald's (Dr. H.) Commentary on the Prophets of the Old Testament. Translated by the Rev. J. F. Smith. Vol. I. General Introduction, Yoel, Amos, Hosea and Zakharya 9—11. Vol. II. Yesaya, Obadya and Mikha. Vol. III. Nahûm, Ssephanya, Habaqqûq, Zachârya, Yéremya. Vol. IV. Hezekiel, Yesaya xl.—lxvi. Vol. V. and last, Haggai, Zakharya, Malaki, Jona, Baruc, Daniel, Appendix and Index. 8vo, cloth. Each 10*s*. 6*d*.

—— **Commentary on the Psalms.** Translated by the Rev. E. Johnson, M.A. 2 vols. 8vo, cloth. Each 10*s*. 6*d*.

—— **Commentary on the Book of Job,** with Translation. Translated from the German by the Rev. J. Frederick Smith. 8vo, cloth. 10*s*. 6*d*.

Falconer (Dr. W.) Dissertation on St. Paul's Voyage from Cæsarea to Puteoli, and on the Apostle's Shipwreck on the Island Melite. 8vo, cloth. 3*s*. 6*d*.

Frankfurter (Dr. O.) Pali Handbook; being (1) A Pali Grammar, (2) Pali Texts, (3) Glossary. 8vo.

Fuerst (Dr. Jul.) Hebrew and Chaldee Lexicon to the Old Testament. 4th Edition, improved and enlarged. Translated by Rev. Dr. Samuel Davidson. Royal 8vo, cloth. 21*s*.

—— Kept also half-bound morocco. 26*s*.

Goldschmidt (H. E.) German Poetry; with the English Versions of the best Translators. Poems of Goethe, Schiller, Freiligrath, Bürger, Heine, Uhland, Körner, &c. &c. Translated by Carlyle, Anster, Blackie, Sir Th. Martin, Shelley, Lord Ellesmere, Lord Lytton, Coleridge, Longfellow, Edgar Bowring, Garnett, &c. 8vo, cloth. 5*s*.

Gostwick (J.) and R. Harrison. Outlines of German Literature. Dedicated to Thos. Carlyle. New Edition. 8vo. 10*s*.

Gotch (Rev. Dr. J. W.) Codex Cottonianus. A Supplement to Tischendorf's Fragments in the Monumenta Sacra. Together with a Synopsis of the Codex. Facsimile. 4to, cloth. 7*s*. 6*d*.

Gould (Rev. S. Baring) Lost and Hostile Gospels. An Account of the Toledoth Jesher, two Hebrew Gospels circulating in the Middle Ages, and extant Fragments of the Gospels of the first Three Centuries of Petrine and Pauline Origin. Crown 8vo, cloth. 7*s*. 6*d*.

Hanson (Sir R. D.) The Apostle Paul and the Preaching of Christianity in the Primitive Church. By Sir R. D. Hanson, Chief Justice of South Australia, Author of "The Jesus of History," &c. 8vo, cloth. (Published at 12*s*.) 7*s*. 6*d*.

Hardy (R. Spence) Manual of Buddhism in its Modern Development. Translated from Cingalese MSS. 2nd Edition, with a complete Index and Glossary. 8vo, cloth. 21*s*.

—— **Eastern [Buddhist] Monachism;** an Account of the Origin, Laws, Discipline, Sacred Writings, &c. &c. of the Order of Mendicants founded by Gotama Buddha. 8vo, cloth. 12*s*.

Hariri. The Assemblies of Al Hariri. Translated from the Arabic, with an Introduction and Notes. Vol. I. Introduction and the first Twenty-six Assemblies. By T. Chenery, Esq. 8vo, cloth. 10*s*.

Hausrath. History of the New Testament Times. The Time of Jesus. By Dr. A. Hausrath, Professor of Theology, Heidelberg. Translated by the Revds. C. T. Poynting and P. Quenzer. 2 vols. 8vo, cloth. 21*s.*

Hemans (Chas. I.) Historic and Monumental Rome. A Handbook for the Students of Classical and Christian Antiquities in the Italian Capital. Crown 8vo, cloth. 10*s.* 6*d.*

—— **History of Mediæval Christianity** and Sacred Art in Italy (A.D. 900—1500). 2 vols. Crown 8vo, cloth. 18*s.*

Higginson (Rev. E.) Ecce Messias: or, The Hebrew Messianic Hope and the Christian Reality. 8vo, cloth. (Published at 10*s.* 6*d.*) 6*s.*

Horne (W.) Religious Life and Thought. By William Horne, M.A., Dundee, Examiner in Philosophy in the University of St. Andrews; Author of "Reason and Revelation." Crown 8vo, cloth. 3*s.* 6*d.*

Huebner (A.) Inscriptiones Brittaniæ Christianæ, with three Geographical Tables. 4to, boards. 16*s.*

Keim's History of Jesus of Nazara. Considered in its connection with the National Life of Israel, and related in detail. Translated from the German by Arthur Ransom. Vol. I. 2nd Edition. Introduction, Survey of Sources, Sacred and Political Groundwork, Religious Groundwork. Vol. II. The Sacred Youth, Self-recognition, Decision. Vol. III. The First Preaching, the Works of Jesus, the Disciples, and Apostolic Mission. Vol. IV. Conflicts and Disillusions, Strengthened Self-confidence, Last Efforts in Galilee, Signs of the approaching Fall, Recognition of the Messiah. Vol. V. The Messianic Progress to Jerusalem, The Entry into Jerusalem, The Decisive Struggle, The Farewell, The Last Supper. (Vol. VI. in the press.) 8vo, cloth. Each 10*s.* 6*d.*

Kuenen (Dr. A.) The Religion of Israel to the Fall of the Jewish State. Translated by A. H. May. 3 vols. 8vo. 31*s.* 6*d.*

—— **Lectures on National Religions and** Universal Religions. (Hibbert Lectures, 1882.) 8vo, cloth. 10*s.* 6*d.*

Laing and Huxley. Pre-Historic Remains of Caithness. By Samuel Laing, Esq., with Notes on the Human Remains by Th. H. Huxley, F.R.S. 150 Engravings. 8vo, cloth. 9*s.*

Lane (E. W.) Arabic-English Lexicon, derived from the best and most copious Eastern Sources. Vols. I. to VI. (to be completed in 8 vols.). Royal 4to. Each 25*s.*

—— Vol. VII. Fascic. I. II. Edited by Stanley Lane-Poole. 4to. Each 6*s.*

Latham (Dr. R. G.) Two Dissertations on the Hamlet of Saxo-Grammaticus and of Shakespear. 8vo. 5*s.*

Lepsius (C. R.) Standard Alphabet for reducing Unwritten Languages and Foreign Graphic Systems to a Uniform Orthography in European Letters. 2nd Edition. 8vo, cloth. 3*s.*

Letters to and from Rome in the Years A.D. 61, 62, and 63. Translated by C. V. S. (by Sir Richard Hanson). Crown 8vo, cloth. 2*s.* 6*d.*

Lindsay (Dr. James, M.A.) The Analytical Interpretation of the System of Divine Government of Moses. 2 vols. 12mo, cloth. 6*s.*

Linguistic Notes on some Obscure Prefixes in Greek and Latin. (4 Parts.) Crown 8vo, cloth. 6*s.* 6*d.*

Macan (R. W.) The Resurrection of Jesus Christ. An Essay in three Chapters. Published for the Hibbert Trustees. 8vo, cloth. 5*s.*

Mackay (R. W.) Sketch of the Rise and Progress of Christianity. 8vo, cloth. (Published at 10*s.* 6*d.*) 6*s.*

Malan (Rev. Dr. S. C.) The Book of Adam and Eve, also called the Conflict of Adam and Eve with Satan. A Book of the early Eastern Church. Translated from the Ethiopic, with Notes from the Kufale, Talmud, Midrashim, and other Eastern works. 8vo, cloth. 7*s.* 6*d.*

Massey (Gerald) A Book of the Beginnings. Containing an Attempt to recover and reconstitute the lost Origines of the Myths and Mysteries, Types and Symbols, Religion and Language, with Egypt for the Mouthpiece and Africa as the Birthplace. 2 vols. Imperial 8vo, cloth. 36*s.*

Milinda Panho, the. Being Dialogues between King Milinda and the Buddhist Sage Nāgasena. The Pali Text, edited by V. Trenckner. 8vo. 21*s.*

—— vide also Pali Miscellany.

Mind, a Quarterly Review of Psychology and Philosophy. Nos. 1—28. 1876-82. 8vo, each 3*s.* Annual Subscription, post free, 12*s.*

Müller (Professor Max) Lectures on the Origin and Growth of Religion, as illustrated by the Religions of India. (Hibbert Lectures, 1878.) 8vo, cloth. 10*s.* 6*d.*

Nibelungenlied. The Fall of the Nibelungers, otherwise the Book of Kriemhild. An English Translation by W. N. Lettsom. Crown 8vo, cloth. 7*s.* 6*d.*

Nicolson (Rev. W. M.) Classical Revision of the Greek New Testament. Tested and applied on uniform Principles, with suggested Alterations of the English Version. Crown 8vo, cloth. 3*s.* 6*d.*

Norris (E.) Assyrian Dictionary. Intended to further the Study of the Cuneiform Inscriptions of Assyria and Babylonia. Vols. I. to III. 4to, cloth. Each 28*s.*

O'Curry (Eng.) Lectures on the Social Life, Manners and Civilization of the People of Ancient Erinn. Edited, with an Introduction, by Dr. W. K. Sullivan. Numerous Wood Engravings of Arms, Ornaments, &c. 3 vols. 8vo. 42*s.*

Oldenberg (Prof. H.) Buddha, his Life, his Doctrine, and his Order. Translated by Dr. Wm. Hoey, B.C.S. 8vo. 18*s.*

—— vide Vinaya Pitakam.

Pali Miscellany, by V. Trenckner. Part I. The Introductory Part of the Milinda Panho, with an English Translation and Notes. 8vo. 4*s.*

Panhellenic Annual for 1880. Edited by S. Parasyrakes. With 21 Illustrations. With Contributions by E. A. Freeman, Professor R. C. Jebb, Professor Ranghabe, the Editor, and many other eminent Greek Scholars. 8vo, cloth, gilt edges. 5*s.*

Peill (Rev. George) The Threefold Basis of Universal Restitution. Crown 8vo, cloth. 3*s.*

Pennethorne (John) The Geometry and Optics of Ancient Architecture, illustrated by Examples from Thebes, Athens and Rome. Folio, with 56 Plates, some in colours. Half morocco. £7. 7*s.*

Pfleiderer (O.) Paulinism: a Contribution to the History of Primitive Christian Theology. Translated by E. Peters. 2 vols. 8vo. 21*s.*

—— **Philosophy of Religion.** Translated by the Rev. Alexander Stewart, of Dundee. (In 3 vols.) Vol. I. 8vo.

Platonis Philebus, with Introduction, Notes and Appendix; together with a Critical Letter on the "Laws" of Plato, and a Chapter of Palæographical Remarks, by the Rev. Dr. Chas. Badham, D.D. 2nd Edition, enlarged. 8vo, cloth. 4*s.*

—— **Euthydemus et Laches,** with Critical Notes and "Epistola critica" to the Senate of the Leyden University, by the Rev. C. Badham, D.D. 8vo, cl. 4*s.*

—— **Convivium (Symposium),** with Critical Notes and an Epistola (de Platonis Legibus) to Dr. Thompson, Master of Trinity College, Cambridge, by the Rev. C. Badham, D.D. 8vo, cloth. 4*s.*

Protestant Commentary, A Short, on the Books of the New Testament: with general and special Introductions. Edited by Professors P. W. Schmidt and F. von Holzendorff. Translated from the Third German Edition, by the Rev. F. H. Jones, B.A. (In 3 vols.) Vol. I. Matthew to Acts. 8vo, cloth. 10*s*. 6*d*.

Quarry (Rev. J.) Genesis and its Authorship. Two Dissertations. 2nd Edition, with Notice of Animadversions of the Bishop of Natal. 8vo. 12*s*.

Reliquiæ Aquitanicæ; being Contributions to the Archæology and Palæontology of Périgord and the adjoining Provinces of Southern France. By Lartet and Christy. Edited by T. Rupert Jones, F.R.S., F.G.S. 87 Plates, 3 Maps, and 130 Wood Engravings. Royal 4to, cloth. £3. 3*s*.

Renan (E.) On the Influence of the Institutions, Thought and Culture of Rome on Christianity and the Development of the Catholic Church. Translated by the Rev. C. Beard. (Hibbert Lectures, 1880.) 8vo, cloth. 10*s*. 6*d*.

Renouf (P. le Page) Lectures on the Origin and Growth of Religion as illustrated by the Religion of Ancient Egypt. (Hibbert Lectures, 1879.) 8vo, cloth. 10*s*. 6*d*.

Reville (Rev. Dr. A.) The Song of Songs, commonly called the Song of Solomon, or the Canticle. Crown 8vo, cl. 1*s*. 6*d*.

Sadi. The Gulistan (Rose-Garden) of Shaik Sadi of Shiraz. A new Edition of the Persian Text, with a Vocabulary, by F. Johnson. Square royal 8vo, cloth. 15*s*.

Samuelson (James) Views of the Deity, Traditional and Scientific: a Contribution to the Study of Theological Science. Crown 8vo, cloth. 4*s*. 6*d*.

Schmidt (A.) Shakespeare Lexicon. A complete Dictionary of all the English Words, Phrases, and Constructions in the Works of the Poet. 2 vols. Imp. 8vo, 30*s*.; cloth, 34*s*.

Schurman (J. G.) Kantian Ethics and the Ethics of Evolution. A Critical Study. (Published by the Hibbert Trustees.) 8vo, cloth. 5*s*.

Seth (A.) The Development from Kant to Hegel, with Chapters on the Philosophy of Religion. (Published by the Hibbert Trustees.) 8vo, cloth. 5*s*.

Sharpe (Samuel) History of the Hebrew Nation and its Literature. With an Appendix on the Hebrew Chronology. 4th Edition, 487 pp. 8vo, cl. 7*s*. 6*d*.

—— **The Decree of Canopus,** in Hieroglyphics and Greek, with Translations and an Explanation of their Hieroglyphical Characters. 16 Plates. 8vo, cloth. 7*s*. 6*d*.

—— **Hebrew Inscriptions from the Valleys** between Egypt and Mount Sinai, in their Original Characters, with Translations and an Alphabet. 2 Parts. 20 Plates. 8vo, cloth. 7*s*. 6*d*.

—— vide also Bible, and Testament.

Sharpe (M.) Old Favourites from the Elder Poets, with a few Newer Friends. A Selection. 418 pp. Crown 8vo, cl. 5*s*.

Smith (Rev. J. F.) Studies in Religion under German Masters. Essays on Herder, Goethe, Lessing, Frank, and Lang. Crown 8vo, cloth. 5*s*.

—— vide Ewald's Prophets and Job.

Sophocles. The Greek Text critically revised, with the aid of MSS., newly collated and explained. By Rev. F. H. M. Blaydes. I. Philoctetes. II. Trachiniæ. III. Electra. IV. Ajax. 8vo, cloth. Each 6*s*.

Spencer (Herbert) First Principles. 5th Thousand, with an Appendix. 8vo. 16*s*.

—— **The Principles of Biology.** 2 vols. 8vo. 34*s*.

—— **The Principles of Psychology.** 4th Thousand. 2 vols. 8vo. 36*s*.

—— **The Principles of Sociology.** Vol. I. 21*s*.

—— **Ceremonial Institutions.** (Principles of Sociology, Vol. II. Part 1.) 8vo. 7*s*.

Spencer (Herbert) Political Institutions. (Principles of Sociology, Vol. II. Part 2.) 8vo. 12*s.*

—— **The Data of Ethics.** Being the First Portion of the Principles of Ethics. 8vo, cloth. 8*s.*

—— **The Study of Sociology.** Library Edition (being the 9th), with a Postscript. 8vo, cloth. 10*s.* 6*d.*

—— **Education:** Intellectual, Moral, and Physical. 8vo, cloth. 6*s.*

—— The same, cheaper Edition, 4th Thousand. 12mo, cloth. 2*s.* 6*d.*

—— **Classification of the Sciences:** to which are added, Reasons for dissenting from the Philosophy of M. Comte. 2nd Edition. 8vo. 2*s.* 6*d.*

—— **Essays:** Scientific, Political, and Speculative. (Being the First and Second Series re-arranged, and containing an additional Essay.) 2 vols. 3rd Thousand. 8vo, cloth. 16*s.*

—— **Essays.** (Third Series.) Including the Classification of the Sciences. 3rd Edition. 8vo. 8*s.*

—— **Descriptive Sociology,** or Groups of Sociological Facts. Compiled and abstracted by Professor D. Duncan, of Madras, Dr. Richard Sheppig, and James Collier. Folio, boards. No. 1. English, 18*s.* No. 2. Ancient American Races, 16*s.* No. 3. Lowest Races, Negritto Races, Polynesians, 18*s.* No. 4. African Races, 16*s.* No. 5. Asiatic Races, 18*s.* No. 6. American Races, 18*s.* No. 7. Hebrews and Phœnicians, 21*s.* No. 8. The French Civilization, 30*s.*

Spinoza. Four Essays by Professors Land, Van Vloten, and Kuno Fischer, and by E. Renan. Edited by Professor Knight, of St. Andrews. Crown 8vo, cloth. 5*s.*

Stephens (George) Old Northern Runic Monuments of Scandinavia and England, now first collected and deciphered. Numerous Engravings on Wood and 15 Plates. Vols. I. and II. Folio. Each 50*s.*

—— Vol. III. (In the Press.)

—— **Macbeth, Earl Siward and Dundee:** a Contribution to Scottish History from the Rune-Finds of Scandinavia. Plates. 4to. 2*s.*

—— **Thunor the Thunderer,** carved on a Scandinavian Font about the year 1000. 4to. 6*s.*

Stokes (Whitley) Old Irish Glossaries. Cormac's Glossary. O'Davoran's Glossary. A Glossary to the Calendar of Oingus the Culdee. Edited, with an Introduction and Index. 8vo, cloth. 10*s.* 6*d.*

—— **Middle-Breton Hours.** Edited, with a Translation and Glossary. 8vo, boards. 6*s.*

—— **The Creation of the World.** A Mystery in Ancient Cornish. Edited, with Translations and Notes. 8vo, cloth. 6*s.*

Strauss (Dr. D. F.) Life of Jesus for the People. The Authorized English Edition. 2 vols. 8vo, cloth. 24*s.*

Sullivan (W. K.) Celtic Studies, from the German of Dr. Hermann Ebel, with an Introduction on the Roots, Stems and Derivatives, and on Case-endings of Nouns in the Indo-European Languages. 8vo, cloth. 10*s.*

Taine (H.) English Positivism. A Study of John Stuart Mill. Translated by T. D. Haye. Crown 8vo, cloth. 3*s.*

Tayler (Rev. John James) An Attempt to ascertain the Character of the Fourth Gospel, especially in its relation to the first Three. 2nd Edition. 8vo, cl. 5*s.*

Testament, The New. Translated by S. Sharpe, Author of "The History of Egypt," &c. 14th Thousand. Fcap. 8vo, cloth. 1*s.* 6*d.*

Thoughts (365) for Every Day in the Year. Selected from the Writings of Spiritually-minded Persons. By the Author of "Visiting my Relations." Printed with red lines. Crown 8vo, cl. 2*s.* 6*d.*

Tien (Rev. A.) The Levant Interpreter: a Polyglot Dialogue-book, in English, Turkish, Modern Greek, and Italian. Crown 8vo. 5*s.*

Turpie (Dr. D. McC.) The Old Testament in the New. The Quotations from the Old Testament in the New classified according to their Agreement with or Variation from the Original: the various Readings and Versions of the Passages, Critical Notes. Royal 8vo, cloth. 12*s.*

—— **Manual of the Chaldee Language:** containing Grammar of the Biblical Chaldee and of the Targums, a Chrestomathy, Selections from the Targums, with a Vocabulary. Square 8vo, cl. 7*s.*

Vinaya Pitakam: one of the principal Buddhist Holy Scriptures. Edited in Pali by Dr. H. Oldenberg. In 5 vols. 8vo. Vol. I. The Mahâvagga. Vol. II. The Cullavagga. Vol. III. The Suttavibhanga, I. (Pârâjika, Samghâdisesa, Aniyata Nissaggiya). Vol. IV. The Suttavibhanga, II. (Mahavibhanga, Bhikkunivibhanga). 8vo. Each 21*s.*

Williams (Rev. Dr. Rowland) The Hebrew Prophets, during the Assyrian and Babylonian Empires. Translated afresh from the Original, with regard to the Anglican Version, with Illustrations for English Readers. 2 vols. 8vo, cloth. 22*s.* 6*d.*

—— **Psalms and Litanies,** Counsels and Collects, for Devout Persons. By Rowland Williams, D.D., late Vicar of Broadchalke, sometime Senior Fellow and Tutor of King's College, Cambridge. Edited by his Widow. Fcap. 4to, cloth extra. 12*s.* 6*d.*

—— **Broadchalke Sermon-Essays** on Nature, Mediation, Atonement, Absolution, &c. Crown 8vo, cloth. 7*s.* 6*d.*

Zeller (Dr. E.) The Contents and Origin of the Acts of the Apostles critically investigated. Preceded by Dr. Fr. Overbeck's Introduction to the Acts of the Apostles from De Wette's Handbook. Translated by Joseph Dare. 2 vols. 8vo, cloth. 21*s.*

WILLIAMS & NORGATE have published the following Catalogues of their Stock.

1. CLASSICAL CATALOGUE. Greek and Latin Classics.
2. THEOLOGICAL CATALOGUE. Including Philosophy and Metaphysics.
3. FRENCH CATALOGUE. General Literature, History, Travels, &c.
4. GERMAN CATALOGUE. General Literature.

* MAP CATALOGUE. Foreign Maps and Atlases.

5. LINGUISTIC CATALOGUE. European Languages.

* ITALIAN CATALOGUE.

* SPANISH CATALOGUE.

6. ORIENTAL CATALOGUE. Oriental Languages and Literature.
7. MEDICAL CATALOGUE. Medicine, Surgery, &c.
8. NATURAL HISTORY CATALOGUE. Zoology, Botany, Geology, Paleontology.
9. NATURAL SCIENCE CATALOGUE. Mathematics, Astronomy, Physics, Mechanics, Chemistry, &c.
10. ART CATALOGUE. Architecture, Painting, Sculpture and Engraving. Books illustrated by Artists.
11. SCHOOL CATALOGUE. Elementary Books, Maps, &c.

C. GREEN AND SON, PRINTERS, 178, STRAND.

www.ingramcontent.com/pod-product-compliance
Lightning Source LLC
Chambersburg PA
CBHW030407170426
43202CB00010B/1525
* 9 7 8 3 3 3 7 2 3 5 8 4 0 *